A Grave Undertaking

Adventures in a Haunted Funeral Home

Richard Estep

Contents

Foreword

When moving into a funeral home, you have certain expectations: leaky ceilings, creepy hallways, loud doors, the general feeling of being haunted. What you *don't* expect is to be welcomed by an established community or such peace in the presence of specters.

Moving in, I had hopes of the house being haunted. I assumed that my family and I would feel unsafe and always uneasy. I had images of a rundown town and home that would leave us regretting every decision we had made so far. What I found was a lively town, and a jaw-dropping house, a house ready and excited to be made a home.

After a short time, I started to experience a lot of paranormal activity, such as slamming doors, yelling, shadows, and loud footsteps in a house only occupied by one human person at the time. The same rang true for my mother. After the idea of us going crazy passed we settled on the obvious...

...ghosts.

To find out more, we started looking into bringing in professionals; people who could really help us. We didn't want to get rid of the ghosts, we wanted to understand them. We didn't have any luck!

Then, Richard Estep approached us about potentially writing a book on the house, and everything fell into place.

Richard and his team came to my house and stayed for a week, doing all types of tests and research. They made a big effort to include my family and I, to make us feel like we were part of the team and to ensure our understanding of what we were dealing with. They taught us about what they were doing, why they were doing it, and how. Richard and his team shared their experiences with us and connected with us. They were the perfect team to guide us on this journey of secrets and lore.

Getting to know him and his team as well as I do now, I have utter faith in Richard's insight. Richard brings such energy and light into every situation he's in, he makes the most of it with the people he's with and he puts his whole heart into whatever he faces. He and his team are a wonderful group, who have helped us to discover many things about our home and its history, all of it curious and strange. I have so much love and respect for Richard and his team along with everything they do.

It would be a gigantic understatement to say I'm looking forward to seeing what they do next. With my whole heart I wish them luck in their next adventure, and I'm ecstatic to hear about what they've found in my home. And why do I feel like we have barely scratched the surface of what's actually going on here?

Noa Blumberg (aka "Monkey")

Introduction

J ust who on Earth would want to buy a haunted funeral home, renovate it, and then live there?

Meet the Blumbergs.

Arryn, aged 45; Heather, "*I'm not going to tell you Richard, and so help me God, I'll have you killed — okay, 48.*" Raff, 21; and his sister, Noa, 15.

Boy, do we have a story to tell you.

If you're familiar with the Blumberg family, you probably first met them, as I did, on television. I was sitting at home one night, idly flicking through channel after channel of the endless streaming morass. Spoiled for choice, and with low expectations, I stopped scrolling when a thumbnail caught my eye. It depicted four people, clearly parents and their two children, standing in front of a distinctly creepy-looking old building.

*The Blumberg family (sans
dogs) outside their dream home.*

Well, creepy is my jam. As a paranormal investigator for almost
thirty years and the author of several books about ghosts and hauntings, I'm intrigued by anything that has a whiff of the supernatural
about it. The title of the show was the final hook: *We Bought a Funeral
Home.*

I pointed the remote, and with one *click,* fired off the first episode.

Hours later, my wife and I were still watching. We were hooked
within minutes. The Blumberg family somehow came across as being
both larger than life and completely genuine, a difficult feat to pull off
on what passes for "reality" television these days. (Pro tip: it helps that
they are *completely* genuine. What you see is what you get).

I have one big complaint about *We Bought a Funeral Home,*
and it's one shared by many people. It's too short. The show is over in
just six episodes, and it left me wanting to see more. (Hey, reputable
TV producers, if you're reading this — renew this show for a second
season!)

I wanted to know more about the family and their adventures
in that shadowy, creaky old funeral parlor. Something else that struck
me was that the ghosts and haunting were a little too peripheral for my
liking. That's not to say that it was a bad choice by the TV company
and the network. Home renovation shows can draw big audiences.
But I was more interested in the spirits which might still linger in that

place than I was in how to put a new kitchen island in. (For balance, I should add that my wife Laura holds exactly the opposite opinion).

By the time the credits rolled after the final episode, I knew that there was so much story still to be told. Selfishly, and perhaps with just a touch of arrogance, I really wanted to be the one to tell it.

I reached out to Heather and introduced myself. She was polite and friendly. I explained who I am, what I do, and that I'd love to help figure out exactly what is going on in her new house. For good measure, I sent her a couple of my books to serve as a kind of calling card. It wasn't long before the Blumbergs made a family decision to allow me to go ahead and write the book you are now either holding in your hands, scrolling through on your digital device, or listening to as it's narrated in the silky-smooth tones of Mr. Josh Heard. (The actual Kiefer Sutherland was out of my price range. He's the next best affordable thing).

Once the green light was given, I wasted no time in assembling a small team of trusted paranormal investigators (not to mention two self-proclaimed weirdos and a dog) with whom I would travel to Canada and investigate the haunting for myself. The adventure that followed was one which I will never forget, and you're about to come along for the ride. You'll be with us every step of the way, as we try to connect with both the living and the dead inside television's most infamous haunted funeral home.

Hang on to your hats, because things are about to get spooky.

Richard Estep

Longmont, Colorado

June 3, 2024

Chapter One

The Dresden Files

S ay the name "Dresden" and one tends to think of Germany, not Canada. The Canadian Dresden is a small agricultural community located in south-western Ontario. For readers from the US, it feels a lot like one of the many farming towns which dot the Midwest. The people are, in my admittedly limited experience, friendly, hardworking, and kind. Dresden is a place which puts its feet up at sunset and relaxes until bedtime. A wild and crazy town, it most definitely is not.

All of which made for a little culture shock for the Blumberg family, when they traded Toronto's big city living to settle down for a life in the country.

It's safe to say that the Blumbergs are not your typical, traditional family. "We're a bunch of weirdos," Heather says without shame or preamble. Raff prefers the term "eccentric." That is, if anything, an understatement.

To use a torturous metaphor, if Halloween went out on a date with *Dia de los Muertos* and had a one-night stand, nine months later (sometime around July 31st) you'd end up with the Blumbergs.

Browsing the property listings one day in 2020, Arryn hit upon an article about a funeral home for sale. The price was right —

$570,000 — and the family was ready for a change of scene. The bigger question became: was rural Ontario ready for *them?*

Almost every town in the world has *that* house...the one the kids talk about in hushed, nervous tones. The place which looks as though there's a specter lurking behind each window, peering back at you as you hurry past. Three floors aboveground, topped by a black wrought-iron fence and a cupola, there's also a basement, a yard — even a swimming pool, surprisingly enough. Not something one would typically associate with a funeral home, I'm sure you'd agree.

The property itself dates back to the 1880s and has served the people of Dresden for over a century. At the time it was put on the market, it was no longer an active funeral home. For Heather and Arryn, it was love at first sight. Their black hearts fell head over heels for the gothic mansion before they even set eyes on the place in person.

After having been deserted for nearly six years, the 12,000 foot, 38-room house would need a fair amount of TLC before becoming livable. In addition to that, Heather had grandiose plans about transforming the huge volume of living space into the home of her dreams. There was a massive amount of potential just waiting for them behind those walls, but it would require a lot of time, money, and sheer hard work to fully realize it.

The Blumbergs were up for the challenge.

Surveys were done. Papers were signed. The deal went through fairly quickly. An agreement was struck up with a TV production company to document the process in the form of a six-part series. They sensed, quite rightly, that not only was there huge entertainment gold to be mined from the family moving in and renovating, but it would also inspire viewers who were looking to make improvements to their own homes.

One of the misconceptions I had while I was watching the show was the assumption that the TV company had probably bought the house for the Blumbergs in order to make the show. In fact, the family had financed the purchase and renovations themselves (although they were paid a fee for starring in it).

Some teenagers would be nervous, if not frightened about moving into an old funeral home. Not so Noa Blumberg, who was about as giddy with excitement as Noa ever gets. I like to think of Noa as being a cross between Yoda, Emily the Strange, and Wednesday Addams, with an approximate age somewhere between 15 and 800 years old. Noa actively *hoped* there would be ghosts in the house, and possibly even some monsters to keep them company.

Neither she nor Raff were prepared for just how big their new home was inside. Stripped of many of the fixtures and fittings of everyday life, the rooms and corridors were a series of wide-open spaces and countless open doors, behind which ...well, we'll get to that.

In many ways, the house was a huge blank slate. In their minds, Heather and Arryn were already filling in the details, mentally superimposing their dream kitchen, living room, and perhaps most importantly a fully stocked wet bar, onto the emptiness.

Noa and Raff (I'd refer to them as "the kids," but either one of them might kill me in my sleep) rushed to pick out their bedrooms. Noa made the third floor her own, whereas Raff laid claim to the basement. It's only appropriate that he have an underground lair; if

Raff wasn't such a kindhearted soul, he'd make a great evil genius in a James Bond movie.

Roaming their new domain and masters of all they surveyed were Satan, a gorgeous Black Lab Retriever, and brothers Pork and Beans, who are both Great Dane siblings. The latter two are all muscle, the type of eating machines that would terrify any potential burglar. Despite his name, Satan, bless his stodgy heart, is a little more on the cuddly side. (As you're almost certainly wondering, I can reveal that the Dark One's name was bestowed by none other than Raff).

It's a truism that moving house is always, at the very least, akin to hell on Earth. Once the Blumbergs and the movers had carted their stuff inside the house, and waved goodbye to the truck, they immediately set about making themselves at home. Unpacking the essentials one item at a time, it wasn't long before they had a makeshift kitchen, living room, and bedroom, with more permanent renovations soon to be underway.

That's when the weirdness started.

It was classic haunted house stuff. Strange noises started most nights after dark. The lights began flickering, then going back to normal. Pork, Beans and Satan developed a habit of staring and growling at what appeared to be empty space, as though they were reacting to something that the human members of the family could not see. This happened frequently on the main staircase, something which would take on new significance in the days ahead.

Could it be that the funeral home was haunted?

Of course, a skeptic would point out that old houses often come with old wiring, and that old wiring causes sometimes lights to flicker. Dogs and cats frequently react to things which seemingly aren't there, although the boys hadn't done that at their last home in Toronto.

Raff was skeptical. A definite non-believer in ghosts, he nonetheless maintained a creditably open mind where the subject was concerned. Ready to be convinced, though it would take some solid evidence to do so. Noa, on the other hand, was an abject believer. She had no trouble whatsoever in accepting the possibility that not everybody (or should that be *every body?*) who had passed through the doors of the funeral home had necessarily left.

Interestingly enough, that also mirrored the views of their parents. Arryn trended toward the skeptical, whereas Heather leaned more toward believing. As is so often the case, the truth could usually be found somewhere in between. It's also important to bear in mind that bias has a tremendous power in and of itself. The funeral home *looked* like it ought to be haunted. The influence that this would exert on the human mind should not be overlooked. Every creaking floorboard might easily be misconstrued as the stealthy tread of a restless soul prowling through the darkness — instead of the entirely natural sounds made by an aged structure settling down at the end of the day. The fact that bats swooped through the floors, dive-bombing the unwary, didn't help matters.

It's also worth pointing out that traditionally, both construction and deconstruction are considered to be triggers and catalysts for paranormal activity. Hauntings which have lain fallow and dormant for years can suddenly flair up when walls are knocked down and the layout of a building is changed. Within days of moving in, the Blumbergs set about smashing through walls with axes and hammers, tearing out drywall and battering the interior into some rough semblance of the way they wanted it to be.

Working on a budget somewhere between $250,000 and $350,000 (it would later expand to $400,000) the Blumbergs auditioned a series of contractors to help them realize their dream. Once the interview process was over, they settled upon Dave.

At first it was slow going, with only incremental process. It takes time to get the various permissions and resources in place that allow a homeowner to make significant changes to a property. The family did what they could, slowly working on turning the house into something more like a home. When the construction crew could finally set to work, things shifted into a higher gear.

There was no shortage of mishaps and bumps along the road. Leaking pipes which almost brought down the ceiling and threatened to saturate the floor beneath when it rained.

Yet stranger things were still to come...

Before we go any further, I should note that every member of the Blumberg family has a creative streak, and each of them expresses it in their own way. For Heather, it's visualizing and designing building interiors. Raff can turn his hand to designing pretty much *anything,* with a flair for art that has to be seen to be believed. Noa writes, draws, and crafts.

Then there's Arryn, who takes a slightly different route. His genius can be found in mixology: the concoction of drinks that are so potent they'll curl your toes, and so palatable that you'll always want more.

With the caveat that we should always drink responsibly, Arryn has graciously agreed to share some of his favorite recipes here within these pages. **Drink them responsibly,** if you choose to make them. Consider them a special feature accompanying this book...a gift from the man himself to help make the rough writing more palatable.

So, with no further ado, here's the man himself giving you three of his favorite cocktails.

Don't say I didn't warn you ;)

Over to you, Arryn...

Chapter Two

Arryn's Adult Beverages - Transparent

Cocktails, unlike baking, can be adjusted to satisfy each drinker's palette, with a substitution of one beverage for another creating a wholly new, unexpectedly marvelous concoction all your own making. So, please take each drink as a guide, not a recipe and don't be afraid of that ancient sherry in the back of the drinks cabinet when you've run out of everything else!

Transparent

1.2 oz Absolut Vodka

2.1.5 oz Hakutsuru Draft Sake Junmai (or another very clean, clear sake that is best served cold)

If you prefer a dryer martini then follow a standard 2:1 ratio but I recommend trying the wetter version to create a wonderful sake forward drink

3.*Add everything to a large heavy shaker ¾ full of ice*

4.*Shake angrily*

5.*Serve in an iced coupe glass, ideally antique (don't bother with straining as the fine ice chips look like diamonds floating)*

Tip - if you forget to chill your glasses before you need to use them, as I always do, then fill each glass with ice and top off with water. By the time you've made your drink they will be nicely cold. Simply discard the icy water and replace it with your freshly made cocktail.

6.*No garnish, unless you have fresh cherry blossoms to hand*

7.*Drink quickly before it warms up*

Chapter Three

"Somebody Likes You..."

No renovation is a cakewalk. When you all but gut a property with a view to completely re-doing it, things become an order of magnitude more difficult. On the plus side, what makes a family like the Blumbergs tear their hair out in the real world also makes for highly entertaining reality television.

In the basement, what was once the embalming area would be transformed into a combination cigar lounge and Prohibition era-style speakeasy. The lift which transported body after body up and down was replaced with a casket...which, when opened, contained a fully stocked wet bar. It's the first mobile, traveling-between-floors bar that I've ever heard of. The casket is real, not a prop. It was purchased from a local undertaker, causing a raised eyebrow when Arryn and Heather revealed their reasons for buying it.

One of the more unusual bars
you'll ever encounter.

Heather's vision was for the Speakeasy to be the social center of
the house, used to entertain friends and visitors without distractions
such as a television to get in the way. A barber's chair behind newly
installed glass doors replaced the table which was once used to embalm
dead bodies.

The Blumbergs and their contractor set about ripping out
extraneous walls, stairs and other parts of the house with gusto. It's
probably no coincidence that the creepy activity in the home seemed
to ramp up at the same time. Shadows were caught moving from the
corner of the eye; the dogs becoming increasingly agitated at thin air,
and still more strange noises quickly became the norm rather than the
exception.

Were the spirits of the funeral home making their presence
known?

In a slightly macabre turn of events, when the family discovered
an industrial-grade cardboard box in the cellar which was once used
to transport a dead body via commercial airline, Heather opted to
clean it up, frame it, and hang it in the hallway to greet future visitors.
Granted, an unusual choice, but it sorta works. At the time of my visit,
I'll discover that it's still there. It's certainly a unique talking point,
though I do recommend not looking *too* closely at some of the wear,
tear...and stains.

Draped with scarlet curtains and fortune telling arcana, stacked with vinyl records and wooden furnishings, the completed Speakeasy is as different from the embalming area as night is to day. The same is true of the parlor (or as Raff likes to call it, "a hallway") which Heather was determined to transform from a bare, wide-open space into a plush green emporium suitable for sitting and lounging in. Buckets of cash, sweat and elbow grease went into the transformation. When the dust settled, I like to think that both Heather and Raff had a valid point of view. Hands down the best feature is a bookcase which swings wide open when a very specific book is pulled open. You half expected to find a pole leading down to the Batcave lurking back behind there.

A bombshell came in the form of an unexpected visitor: a local lady who came bearing both pie and a ghost story concerning the funeral home. She had lived in the house back in the 1940s and was well acquainted with one of the resident phantoms, a fair-haired apparition named The Lady in Blue — so named because of the flowing blue gown she wears. The ghost was most often seen standing partway up the winding master staircase, in front of the colorful tinted glass window. She was accompanied by the ghost of a small white dog.

According to the visitor, the Lady in Blue was a friendly spirit, albeit an uncommunicative one. She simply stood there, never uttering a word. All of which begs the question...who exactly is she?

The Blumbergs took the news in their stride. Heather and Noa are believers. Raff and Arryn are not. Without actually passing the Lady in Blue on the staircase someday, it's unlikely that either of the men in the house would change their minds on the subject...or so I thought then. I would later come to learn that both Raff and Arryn were open-minded skeptics, with Raff in particular willing to pitch in and try his hand at some paranormal field research.

Noa, on the other hand, jumped in with both feet from the outset. Hearing the firsthand account of a specific ghost haunting her new home, she immediately set about trying to uncover the identity of the mysterious Lady in Blue. A few days later, a set of night vision goggles and an EMF (electromagnetic field) meter turned up in the mail. Noa was building herself a ghost hunting kit.

It's worth considering whether we're dealing with an intelligent or a residual haunting. The literature of the paranormal is replete with similar cases of enigmatic figures haunting old, historic residences. More often than not, they seem completely unaware of the living human beings that encounter them. When spoken to, they don't reply. Instead, they simply stare into the distance, not acknowledging the presence of the eyewitness in any way. This is a residual haunting, an after-echo of days gone by. Such apparitions are no more self-aware than the moving images of people that walk across your television screen.

Intelligent hauntings, on the other hand, behave and interact...well, intelligently. These seem to be some form of disembodied consciousness, or at the very least, a fragment of one. Whether these are the spirits of dead humans or something else entirely remains a matter of debate among members of the paranormal community. Some of the wilder theories involve time travel and extra-dimensional beings, to name just two. One thing is for certain, however: when I get to the Blumberg home in person, my team and I will find out that both types of haunting co-exist there, side by side.

Determined to get to the bottom of the mystery, Noa met with a local historian named Marie, in order to gather more information about the house. As the historian laid it all out for her, listing some of the key personalities who had lived in the house, Heather sat alongside her, nodded and drank coffee.

The historian produced a treasure trove of information, much of it drawn from the land registry. The story began with a boat captain named Edward Huston, who built the home in the 1880s and subsequently lost it due to bankruptcy. In 1901 came Daniel Venning Hicks, an insurance agent and the son of Dresden's Mayor. He lived in the house for less than a decade. Incidentally, Daniel Hicks' father met a tragic and untimely end in 1910 during a gas-fueled explosion in town. According to the Brantford Weekly Expositor newspaper's December 29, 1910, edition (*"One Man Killed in Dresden Explosion"*) Mr. Hicks was killed instantly, crushed by a rain of flying bricks. Others were injured, but he bore the brunt of the blast.

The list of owners went on and on, up to and beyond the property becoming an active funeral home, but frustratingly, the records only listed the males, and not their spouses. This reflected the inherent gender inequalities of those times and made potential identification all the more difficult. Undeterred, Noa and her mother took a field trip to the local cemetery. Armed with the names of those male owners, they set out to track down their graves and thereby shed some light on their wives. Unfortunately, their search turned out to be fruitless...but there was no way that Noa was giving up that easily.

Looking for paranormal investigators on the Internet (without letting anybody know about it first) Noa invited in a husband-and-wife team who lived relatively close by. The couple duly arrived and set about...investigating.

It's at this point that I must declare a bias. Every paranormal investigator has their own way of working, and I'm no exception to that. We all have our own dos, don'ts, and individual research methodologies. Nobody in the field can agree on what constitutes valid evidence and what doesn't. It's a chaotic mishmash of personalities with conflicting viewpoints. As such, I want to be clear that I am in no way trash talking the lady and gentleman that Noa brought. Their methods clearly work for them, and that's all there is to it. My own manner of conducting an investigation differs significantly from theirs and will be outlined later in this book. The reader is invited to make up their own minds regarding its value, or lack thereof.

After a brief introduction, Noa gave a brief overview of the haunting so far. Holding up a rosary, the male investigator declared: "Without this, we have no protection against evil." Right out of the gate, they focused their attention on the part of the staircase haunted by the Lady in Blue, which makes sense. He employed a Mel Meter, a device used to measure electromagnetic energy and temperature. As the readings increased further up the staircase, the female investigator announced that "Somebody is with us."

The next device taken out of their tool kit was a Rem Pod, similar to a theremin. It generates a field that, when broken by physical proximity or certain types of electromagnetic energy such as radio waves, emits a warbling electronic sound and causes a bank of lights to flash. In my experience, the big problem with Rem Pods is that they can be triggered by walkie talkies and vehicle mounted radios such as those mounted on fire engines, ambulances, and police cruisers, to name just three. This Achilles' Heel can be surmounted by placing the Rem Pod in a Faraday Cage, an enclosure which can be bought commercially or constructed very cheaply. In this case, the investigators just sat the Rem Pod on the window ledge and left it unshielded.

The Rem Pod failed to alarm. It sat there silently, just doing its thing. The family and their guests relocated to the newly-renovated Speakeasy, which we would later prove to be one of the most haunted parts of the house — small wonder, given its former status as the embalming area. As their equipment beeped and flashed, the ghost hunters declared that the ghosts were at different places in the room...at one point, in the barber chairs in the cigar lounge...the next, over by the casket bar. Certainly, the Rem Pod was more active in the speakeasy than it was on the staircase.

The investigators equated the increasing readings with the presence of spirits. "Somebody likes you," the man declared, seeing energy levels rising in Raff's vicinity. Whether or not there was an artificial source of electromagnetic energy, such as a power conduit or electrical appliance, did not seem to be taken into account. It's fair to say that any degree of skepticism concerning the readings was in short supply. The female investigator confirmed that "they" — meaning the spirits, presumably — were present in the room at that time.

Once the investigation was complete, Raff had not been swayed very far from their skeptical viewpoints, though he admitted that some of what happened was on the peculiar side. Arryn, on the other hand, was even less convinced than he had been before.

(In fairness to the guest investigators, it must be borne in mind that, although it's called "reality television," what you actually see on TV is a carefully edited version of what actually happened. Sometimes, context can be lost in the service of telling a story, and I'd like to give the couple the benefit of the doubt).

The investigators sent the Blumbergs a series of thermal images which they believed to show "anomalies," and some hard to hear potential EVPs. One might have been the word *mummy*. Embodying the typical response to such recordings, Heather and Noa sided with the investigators, believing that the word was clearly audible against the hiss and crackle of the background noise. Arryn, on the other hand, couldn't hear it at all. Once again, the believers and the skeptics stuck to their opposing views.

They ultimately concluded that the funeral home was haunted by "many spirits," and no matter what anybody might think of their evidence, it would certainly make sense for a building which has such ties with death to remain connected with the dead in more ways than one.

Whatever the case may be, it only makes me want to investigate the place in person even more than I already did.

Chapter Four

Arryn's Adult Beverages - Classic Red

C **lassic Red**

1. *1.5 oz Grey Goose Vodka*

2. *0.5 oz Kirsch Dry Schloss Oberandritz*

3. *0.25 oz Dolin Vermouth De Chambery Dry AOC*

4. *Bar spoon liquor from maraschino cherries (supermarket ones give a fantastic color and classic flavor)*

5. *2-3 drops Peychaud's Bitters*

6. *Add everything to a heavy shaker ¾ full of ice*

7. *Shake with gusto*

8. *Strain into a chilled long stemmed small port glass, something delicate and vintage*

(There is nothing like sipping a heady mix of classic cherry flavors from a small vintage glass to bring out a nostalgic mood).

9. *Garnish with a maraschino cherry*
10. *Enjoy as if it's a cold night in the old country*

Chapter Five

Doppelganger

While one can debate the results of the paranormal investigators' visit to their heart's content (temperature anomaly or simply a heating pipe?), the mystery of the Lady in Blue still endures. Noa was determined to put a name to this enigmatic specter. Working her way through the Huston family tree, the youngest Blumberg turned her eye to Olivia Huston, the wife of Edward, and their daughter Josephine. Neither died in the house, and so Noa eliminated them as potential candidates.

On this point, she and I would disagree. Although conventional wisdom holds that a person must die in a place in order to haunt it, in actuality, that isn't always true. A case in point: for several years, I gave ghost tours at an infamously haunted hotel in the Rocky Mountains. Its uppermost floor was reputed to be the most haunted. The laughter of children was often heard there, along with the running footsteps of child-sized feet. Some even reported seeing apparitions of ghostly children playing in the halls and rooms. During the hotel's early years, that particular floor was the dormitory in which kids and the nannies who looked after them lived, played and slept. Yet according to a thorough search of the hotel records, no child ever died there throughout its entire history. Why, then, were the phenomena all child-like in nature?

It may well be that this particular haunting was born not from trauma and pain, but from happiness...that it was a lingering after-echo of those long, joyful summer holidays which turned out to be the happiest days of those children's lives. Perhaps that joy left behind a kind of psychic residue, one which can still be experienced more than a century later. This was primarily a residual haunting, one without intelligence or awareness, and therefore one without a death on site as its root cause.

By the same token, could the Lady in Blue simply have been a woman who had lived at the house, moved elsewhere, but left a part of herself behind somehow? It's certainly worth considering — as is the possibility that there might be something more sinister at work...

Ladies in blue dresses aren't the only apparitions to be seen at Chez Blumberg. According to the folklore of ghosts and hauntings, a *doppelganger* is the phantom of a living human being — their double, if you will. They're often exact visual replicas, though some variations of the lore state that there's sometimes just a single detail that isn't correct.

My own doppelganger was spotted on the upper cell block of the old Teller County Jail in Cripple Creek, Colorado, during a ghost hunt event. While I was sitting safely ensconced behind iron bars in one of the cells, with a colleague standing in the doorway, another investigator clearly saw me standing outside on the gantry. He was considerably shaken when he discovered that I hadn't left my cell the entire time.

Tradition holds that if you should encounter your own doppelganger, then death shall imminently befall you. It is perhaps for this reason that such entities are thought to be evil versions of their living counterparts...which made it all the more concerning when Dave, the Blumbergs' contractor, saw what he was convinced to be Arryn on the side porch of the funeral home one evening. Whoever it was, it most definitely wasn't Arryn, who hadn't gone out there at all that night...not least because there were safety concerns about the structural instability of the porch, and he didn't fancy a broken leg or two.

Even if Arryn *had* wanted to hang out on the porch, to do so would have been extremely difficult. Behind the door which led out to it were stacks of furniture and other household objects, effectively blocking it off from the outside world. While it would have been possible to haul oneself up onto the porch from the outside, it would have taken a fair amount of effort, and again ran the risk of making the entire structure collapse.

Upon comparing times with Arryn, it was determined that Dave had seen the Arryn-alike after Arryn had already gone to bed for the night. None of the security cameras were set off.

In Heather's view, this was a ghost.

In Arryn's...*meh*. It was just one of those things.

After doing a little digging, the Blumbergs hit upon an alternative explanation. Rather than being Arryn's doppelganger, the man on the porch also bore a striking resemblance to the bushy-bearded

Daniel Hicks, former patriarch of the house. The contractor definitely thought this was the person he saw.

In the meantime, Noa's quest to identify the Lady in Blue was gaining traction. She's convinced that the answer may lie with the Clark family, former residents of the funeral home, who agreed to speak with Noa, Raff and their parents. During a Zoom video call, the Clarks dropped a bombshell: in 1936, their great aunt Gertrude had fallen down that very same staircase and had died when she reached the halfway stage...almost exactly where the apparition has been sighted.

So, there we have it. The sudden and traumatic death of a woman in very close proximity to the place at which the Lady in Blue has been seen. As an explanation for this particular aspect of the haunting, it's hard to deny.

All due credit to Noa, who refused to give up, gnawing away at her research like a dog with a bone. What an exceptional piece of research on her part. She would be a genuine asset to any paranormal research team.

By the end of their first, and sadly so far, the only season of *We Bought a Funeral Home,* the Blumberg family had made significant strides in renovating their new home. It was far from finished, however, and by the time my team of paranormal investigators and I packed our backs for the journey north, it remained a glorious, spectacular work in progress.

In terms of the haunting, there were at least two distinct apparitions for us to look out for — the Lady in Blue and the Man on the Porch — and a plethora of alleged phenomena to be tested and explained...if explanations could indeed be found.

We would soon learn that investigating this particular haunting would be like peeling an onion. Getting to the bottom of one layer would only reveal another one, which in turn needed to be peeled back, only to reveal another, and another and another...

I had no idea when I picked up my passport, hefted one suitcase full of clothes alongside another packed with ghost hunting equipment, and set out for Denver International Airport, that I was heading for one of the most intriguing and colorful cases of my career.

Chapter Six

Arryn's Adult Beverages - Twisted

*T*wisted

1. *2 oz Jose Cuervo Especial Gold (keep the good stuff to drink straight over ice)*

2. *0.5 oz Grand Marnier (I prefer Grand Marnier to Cointreau for a more sophisticated finish)*

3. *2 oz Mosambi - Sweet Lime - Dabur Real Fruit Power (best to look in your local Indian specialty store or Amazon)*

4. *0.5 oz fresh squeezed lime juice (vary how much lime depending on how sour you like it)*

5. *2-3 drops Fee Brothers West Indian Orange Bitters*

6. *Small pinch of Maldon salt (do NOT skip this step)*

(If you don't have Maldon, use another mild high-quality finishing salt, none of that iodized table salt rubbish).

7. *Throw it all in a big shaker full of ice*

8. *Shake until your hands are freezing*

9. *Half-rim a chilled retro coupe glass with Tajin Clasico Seasoning*

10. *When you are squeezing the limes, use a discarded lime half to rub round half of the glass's rim then run it through Tajin seasoning. Pouring the seasoning into a small bowl or plate makes this easy.*

11. *Pour into a chilled retro coupe glass, this drink is more fun when treated as a sipping cocktail than a traditional margarita*

12. *Drink without sharing*

Chapter Seven

Northward Bound

When I set out to investigate a haunted location, I generally work with a small group of trusted fellow investigators and friends. They're usually either people with whom I've investigated in the past, or acquaintances who come highly recommended from my friends and peers.

Rob is part of a small Iowa-based team named Paranormania. When he's not creeping around dark and haunted places, or earning a living at his day job, he's the official merchandise guru for a band. An ever-present hangdog expression and feigned air of cynicism can't effectively hide one of the biggest hearts and sideways senses of humor I know. He's usually seen sporting aviator shades and a baseball cap, though on one particularly memorable adventure in Tombstone, Arizona, he picked up a full-length black duster and circular-brimmed hat. The look he was going for might best be described as "gunslinger." In reality, he was immediately mistaken for a rabbi. Such is Rob's luck sometimes.

I've worked with Stephen and our mutual friend Jill numerous times in the past. An ordained priest who has performed several exorcisms, Stephen is a musician and music teacher by vocation. Both he and Jill, who's a former computer programmer living her best life in early retirement, have some degree of sensitivity to things of a ghostly nature, in addition to being solid technical investigators. They live fairly close to me in Colorado, but we've traveled to locations both far flung within the US and overseas, such as the south of England.

Brad and Tim are a real pair of characters, who are so funny, a novelist couldn't make them up. Lifelong friends, they live in the upper peninsula of Michigan — which makes them so-called "Yoopers." Tim works in the radio broadcasting field, and Brad runs a very successful retail business. In addition to investigating claims of ghosts and hauntings, the dynamic duo run the wildly popular Michigan Paranormal Convention, which is held each summer in Sault St. Marie. This will be our first time investigating together. I've heard very positive things about their expertise and professionalism while on the job. They'll also turn out to be an absolute blast to travel and hang out with. To this day, Brad has developed a habit of texting me early morning memes that are in such poor taste, they'd make a Marine blush and probably put him on several government agency watch lists.

Joining us for a short time only, due to professional commitments, is Jim. He's a fellow paramedic, who also lives in Michigan. When he isn't taking care of sick people, he's teaching others how to do that very thing. This is my first time investigating with him as well. He's a little more reserved than the zany Brad and Tim, but no less fun for that.

*Jim looks on while Stephen
make a friend.*

Lastly, there will be three special guests arriving part way through our time at the funeral home later in the week. We'll get to them in due course.

It's a seasonably mild day in May 2023 when Stephen, Jill and I fly into Detroit. We meet Rob at the airport, and after collecting our luggage — our cases have so much paranormal research equipment in them that they look like they belong to the Unabomber — we pick up a rental car and hit the road. Our destination: the Canadian border. Jill drives. It isn't long before we're taking Exit 192B, which is imaginatively signposted *Bridge to Canada.*

Crossing the Detroit River via the Ambassador Bridge in Hubbard-Richard puts us in that nebulous no man's land between the United States and its cousin to the north. There's a tailback of cars waiting to get across. Jill steers into what looks like shortest line, which is still moving with painstaking slowness, and the four of us settle in for a few rounds of "guess which one's the drug smuggler?" Some of the neighboring vehicles look distinctly suspicious, as do their drivers, at least one of whom is drenched in sweat, pale, and gripping the steering wheel with apparent, white-knuckled terror.

"Your business in Canada?" a bored-sounding immigrations officer asks us.

"Writing a book," I reply with candor. Scanning our passports, he hands them back to us and waves us through. Just like that, we're across the border in Windsor, which is fairly populous and built up. Not for long, however, as Jill is taking no prisoners behind the wheel.

As soon as we're out of the suburbs, our surroundings become increasingly rural. It's a straight shot east along Ontario's Highway 401, then we hook northeast past Chatham, a place we're going to get to know quite well over the course of the next few days. A succession of back roads takes us through farming country, with barns and the occasional house dotting the roadside at irregular intervals. It reminds me a lot of the British countryside in winter. Rob's probably thinking the same thing about the American Midwest. It has a sparse beauty that has to be seen to be appreciated.

After a pit stop at a Tim Hortons, at which we also stock up on enough caffeine to resuscitate a cadaver that's been dead for a week and also rendezvous with Jim, we roll into Dresden early in the afternoon. It's exactly as we've been given to expect from the TV show, a small town that's perhaps one size too big for everybody to know everybody else by name, but it's pretty close. There's a road sign pointing the way toward our final destination — pun very much intended...

...and there it is. The funeral home looks exactly as it does on television, albeit a little less sinister. Perhaps that has something to do with the lack of creepy mood music playing in the background. It's located right in the middle of a residential neighborhood. The four of us get out of the car and stretch, a chorus of middle-aged groans and moans signifying that the ghosts of our youth are making their presence known. There was a time when I could get out of a car without making any kind of noise at all. That time, in case you're interested, was called the 1990s.

I'm in something of a foul mood, if the truth be told. My beloved cat, Stig, was put to sleep yesterday after a short but fierce struggle with illness. Losing a pet always rips my heart out. No matter how many fur babies you lose over the years (and I'm fifty, so it's been a *lot*) it never gets any easier, and that's a Stig-shaped void in my heart today that's dragging me down. Fortunately, I'm about to get a high concentration dose of doggy time, and that, along with the days and nights of paranormal investigation, will turn out to be exactly the tonic that I need.

One look at this magnificent house, however, and all of our assorted aches and pains are gone, replaced with sheer excitement and enthusiasm for what lies ahead. Ringing the doorbell results in a series of deep, throaty barks, followed by the stampeding of three sets of heavy paws. Satan, Pork and Beans are instantly at the door, barking at us from behind the glass.

Noa is still in school, and Raff is away somewhere doing Raff-like things, but Heather and Arryn immediately set about making us welcome. They're every bit as friendly and charming as we've seen on TV. In fact, this is going to be an ongoing theme during our stay. It's a little bit surreal to be talking with people to whom you're a complete stranger, but conversely, you feel as if you know them because you've spent three hours of your life watching them on television. It's a bizarre kind of cognitive dissonance, and one that will only dissipate after a day or two spent in their company. The three boys get petted; ear and chin scratches being handed out with wild abandon by the four of us. Enthusiastically wagging tails smack at our legs with a regular thump as we're led toward the living room.

Just like the exterior, the ground floor of the house is almost exactly as we remember it from the show. At the top of the stairs is Arryn's office, where he handles his day job and presumably refines his plans for world domination.

Continuing on, the wood-paneled entryway has been painted a deep maroon/ burgundy color. Tree branches lining either side of the hallway form an arch under which visitors must pass. A white rabbit peeks out at us from behind a rock. There's a very Lewis Carroll vibe going on. There, still in its glass case, is the wall-mounted body carton that was used to transport human remains to the funeral home from overseas. I try not to think too much about the dark brownish liquid stains which discolor the sturdy cardboard. The name of its occupant is handwritten on it, though I shall not list it here out of respect for the deceased's next of kin.

There's a staircase on our right, spiraling up toward the second floor. A gorgeous woodland mural decorates the wall bordering the stairs, an explosion of lush greens interspersed with trees, butterflies, and other critters. Six electric candles glitter from an opulent chandelier. I pause for a moment at the foot of the steps, staring up at the multicolored stained-glass window. There's no sign of the Lady in Blue, and none of the dogs are paying it much attention. I can't help but wonder whether she'll put in an appearance during our stay.

In the Chapel, as the living room and lounge area is now called, the color scheme changes...and frankly, I have to ask Heather what that type of paint is called, because when it comes to decorating and design, I'm an absolute Philistine. She tells me it's a custom mix of deep black with a velvety finish. The plush leather couch is insanely comfortable. Cue yet more groans and gasps as we sit down, already recovering from our marathon trek of around 100 feet from the parked car.

Stephen has no sooner taken a seat than Pork is in his face, slathering him in drooling love and affection with his sandpaper-rough tongue. For his part, Stephen is all too happy to reciprocate. All of my friends are dog people. If they weren't, I doubt that we'd be friends in the first place.

"Thank you," he says, reaching down to rub the giant furry tummy. (Pork's, not his own). In response, the tail wagging reaches fever pitch. Stephen and Pork have both made a friend for life in one another.

"The kids will be here later," Heather tells me, before giving us a potentially libelous run-down on their personalities. Raff, she says, is "super laid back and easy going. It's almost impossible to upset him. As for Noa...well, let's just say when we were filming the show, the production crew learned very early on that they needed to cut Noa's mic at all times."

"Why?"

"Because she swears like a trucker..." Heather begins counting off reasons on the fingers of one hand. "She'll call you on your shit the very *second* that she sees you...oh, and she never forgives. *Ever.* Once you've crossed her, you're done. She's cute as a button, but she. Will. *Cut You.*"

In the blink of an eye, our collective vision of Noa Blumberg has morphed from that of a sweet yet sassy teenager to something more akin to what John Wick became fifteen minutes into the first movie. Perhaps with a slightly higher body count.

Arryn is a business consultant. Heather's built a career in management for several major companies that you've almost certainly heard of but that I won't name here. Raff and his business partner Doc, who also has a room here in the basement, make a living by rendering graphics for film and TV productions.

Our talk turns to the subject of paranormal activity inside the house. Since production on *We Bought a Funeral Home* wrapped, the Blumbergs have continued to work on other rooms within the cavernous house. Sometimes an entire week will go by without anything of a ghostly nature happening. Then, just like waiting for a bus to turn up, two or three bizarre things will occur in a short space of time, leaving Heather and Noa scratching their heads, while Arryn and Raff remain cheerfully but resolutely skeptical.

It's a big house to keep clean, and so the Blumbergs hired a lady to help with the housework. Last week, she experienced the doors in the basement opening and closing by themselves. Neither Raff nor Doc, both of whom live down there, was in residence at the time.

In addition to the doors, the cleaner heard the sound of a man's voice loudly calling out something intelligible from elsewhere inside the house. Arryn was in his office at the time, working away quietly. He isn't in the habit of bellowing randomly into thin air, so whoever it was, Arryn wasn't to blame.

"We have two separate and distinct female voices that we hear within the house," Heather goes on. "One of them screams as though she's in distress. The other shouts the word *Hello.*"

Whenever somebody answers, there's never a response. Once again, as I make a note of this, I also ask myself the question: are these auditory phenomena interactive or residual in nature? Is there any kind of intelligence behind them, one that we might communicate with during our investigation?

Whichever is the case, the seemingly disembodied male voice is new.

Stephen asks about timing, trying to identify any potential pattern to the voices. We're told that they occur at all hours of the day and night, from three in the afternoon to three o'clock in the morning, without any obvious rhyme or reason.

By far the most common disturbance is phantom footsteps, which also occur around the clock. They come right through the area in which we're now sitting, the former parlor, and tromp their way up the spiral staircase to the second floor, then proceed down the hallway and climb the steps to the third floor, to what were probably once the quarters for servants and "the help."

I'm particularly interested in the apparition that may have been Daniel Hicks. It turns out that this particular phantom has also been seen lurking around the outside of the house by one of the neighbors, which means that there are now at least two independent eyewitnesses who have caught sight of the man. Whatever else he may be, we can probably rule out the possibility of it being a hallucination or trick of the light.

The Clark family suffered at least one death during their tenure inside the home: Gertrude, who fell down the staircase to her death, and remains the prime candidate to be the Lady in Blue.

Now it's Rob's turn to get some love, as Beans plants his head in his lap and demands attention. He receives it in abundance. Rob's a sucker for an adorable doggy face and sets about fussing the giant fur monster while still keeping an ear on the conversation.

Other deaths are associated with the house. Tragically, a male occupant is said to have taken his own life in a room on the second floor. It was a death by hanging. There are anecdotal reports from residents of Dresden that a small number of people died while attending viewings, presumably killed due to the intense emotional stress brought upon by grief. Heather has been stopped several times while going about her business in the town, only to be told by somebody about a relative of theirs who dropped dead inside the funeral home back in the day. It's a macabre and surreal experience, yet one that she has grown used to.

I'm not a sensitive person, in the psychic sense of the term — I leave that to Stephen and Jill — but the atmosphere inside this house feels very warm and welcoming to me. It's homely, for want of a better word. If you didn't know the truth, you'd never realize you were sitting in what was once a funeral home, occupying the very same space in which the bereaved would once stand to view the bodies of their dead loved ones for the final time. I could quite happily curl up on this couch and take a nap, if I wasn't so excited for the adventure that is about to begin.

"We've never really felt creeped out," Heather reveals when I mention this to her. "Yes, it's a very big house, and after dark your imagination can go into overdrive...but I've rarely been really scared to be here."

"Rarely?" That gives me pause.

"There are a handful of exceptions," she admits. "There have been several occasions on which we've heard these *very* heavy footsteps up above us. It only ever happens when either me or Noa are in the house alone."

I make a note of that, too. One way to look at it is fairly sinister: why wait until there's a female in the house all by herself? But then, an alternative perspective is that the phenomenon takes place only when there's a *believer* in the house by themselves. Gender may be entirely irrelevant in this instance. There's a commonly accepted hypothesis that the presence of skeptics can sometimes act as a sort of psychic dampener, throwing a wet blanket on any paranormal activity which might otherwise be taking place.

The footsteps stomp across the second floor, thudding across the ceiling, and then begin to slowly descend the master staircase.

Now, Heather and Noa are both strong and courageous women. They aren't easily shaken by...well, pretty much anything. Yet each time this happened to them, they left the house. Frankly, I don't blame them at all. Unless ghosts and hauntings are something you're very familiar with, part of your everyday wheelhouse, paranormal activity can be very unnerving indeed. A case in point is my young brother, a decorated combat veteran who isn't afraid of anything in this world that he can punch, kick, or shoot. After spending ten minutes in one of the UK's most haunted houses with me — the infamous 30 East Drive in Pontefract, also known as the "Black Monk House," his heart rate and blood pressure had both skyrocketed. Fear can affect the strongest of people in different ways.

Beans has now transferred his affections to Stephen. As the inevitable snuggle fest kicks in, I can't help thinking that the pair of them looks like the worst 1970s-era cop buddy crime-fighting duo ever: Bean and The Priest. Maybe we can make a TV pilot show and sell it to Discovery Plus.

One thing we're noticing about the Blumberg home is that it isn't a particularly noisy house. This is surprising, given its age. Most houses creak as the day goes on, with the changes in temperature causing expansion and contraction within the structure. Not so this one, not even at night when the air cools significantly. Contraction-induced creaking floorboards are often mistaken for ghostly footsteps, which is one reason why so many of them are reported after dark — also a time when the lengthening shadows bring to mind thoughts of ghosts and things that go bump in the night. There's a psychological component to any haunting, and we're still assessing how much of that might be at play here in Dresden.

Sticking with the auditory phenomena, on several occasions the family has heard the sound of music drifting up from the old basement

— what's now known as the Pink Room, which is located at the back of the house. Notably, the music is only ever heard in the early hours of the morning, after midnight and before dawn — most commonly between 2am and 4am. The fact that the music is always heard within a very narrow time window makes me think it's residual, rather than intelligent in origin, but it certainly bears further investigation.

"There's also sounds like two or three male voices in conversation," Heather tells us. "You can never hear what they're talking about — the words are indistinct — but it sounds just like a small group of guys chatting."

We're also very interested in the behavior of Pork, Beans and Satan as it pertains to the haunting. Heather gives us more information.

"They will stand in the parlor, and either look up at the stairs or back towards the Pink Room. Their hackles go up and they start to growl. I'm terribly insomniac, so I'm usually up and about in the wee small hours of the morning. That's why I notice so much of this stuff."

What does she make of the flickering lights? How much is simply attributable to old wiring, as opposed to a potentially paranormal cause?

"The lights don't flicker," she corrects me. "They switch themselves on and off. As in, you'll switch off the lights and leave the room to go and do something. When you come back, they've been switched back on again."

We're not talking about electrical brownouts in old wiring here. The switch is being physically flipped while the room is completely unoccupied. That's far harder to explain away conventionally.

Getting to my feet, I drift over to the nearest light switch and examine it thoughtfully. I'm interrupted when Heather offers to give us all the grand tour. Arryn, who's still on the clock, heads back into his office.

"We'll start at the top and work our way down, if that's okay?"

All five of us nod agreement. We're just so thrilled to be walking through the house that four of us have seen and fallen in love with on television. (Stephen is the only one who has very deliberately not watched the show, in order to avoid biasing himself prior to coming here).

As we climb the stairs, something familiar catches my eye. A Corellian freighter that's universally familiar to everybody, the *Millennium Falcon* from *Star Wars*. This is the Lego Ultimate Collector Series version, 7,541 bricks of Lego-ey goodness. It's sitting on a side table. I have the same kit at home, living proudly on the mantelpiece above the TV. If I'd been in any doubt whatsoever that the Blumbergs might be my kind of people, they've now been totally and utterly dispelled.

"We're massive nerds," Heather confirmed as we keep on going up. "Noa built that kit all by herself when she was just ten."

I let out a low whistle. Building the kit was fun but also a gigantic pain in the arse. There were parts which challenged me, and I'm fifty. For a ten-year-old to do it is no small achievement. It took Noa months to complete. It took me more than a year. The less said about that, the better.

The staircase deposits us on the third-floor landing. It's not quite the highest point of the house, but it is the uppermost residential part. A tighter, narrower set of stairs goes on up to the Widow's Walk, a platform atop the roof which supports a glass-windowed cupola. It's basically an enclosed terrace with incredible views out over the town of Dresden. Interestingly enough, the term "Widow's Walk" may be something of a misnomer. The commonly held belief involves the fact that these architectural features are commonly seen on the east coast of the United States, and other places near the sea. According to legend, they were most popular in houses owned by sea captains and naval officers. When the sailor in question was away at sea, his wife or sweetheart could climb the steps up to the top of the house and watch for her beau to return from the sea. A life on the ocean can be a hazardous one, even today, and was even more so back then. Not all of those men came back, in which case their unsuspecting widows would prowl the Widow's Walk each day, watching for the return of a ship that might never again return to port.

It's a very romantic story, yet there's also a more prosaic explanation for building a Widow's Walk: it was a convenient place for putting out chimney fires. Some homeowners stored containers of water and sand up there, and in the event of their chimney getting out of control, they could rush up there and dump their contents on the blaze in time to save the house from burning down.

Dresden isn't close enough to Lake Huron and Lake Erie to need a Widow's Walk for maritime purposes, but the Sydenham River is close by. The former funeral home was owned by at least one sailor — Edward Huston, who built the property in the first place. These walks were sometimes built as a display of ostentation by the rich ("Hey, look how well off we are!") and could serve as a relaxing place for the homeowner to get away from it all and unwind in the fresh air, all while taking in an inspiring view.

We climb up the ladder and carefully clamber onto the roof. If I lived here, I'd put a chair and small table up on the Widow's Walk and spend hours up here, just reading and enjoying the solitude. Looking out over the rooftops, I can see a nearby park, and houses all around. The library is just a few blocks away, along with some of the town's restaurants and stores.

It's peaceful, with nothing more than a light breeze rustling through the trees. In true Blumberg fashion, the black wrought-iron spiky fence which borders the upper tier of the roof threatens to impale anybody who might slip and fall.

Once everybody has gotten a chance to soak in the rarefied air up here, we return to the third floor for our tour. As with most comparable residences, this would have most likely have been the servant's quarters back in the day. In the late 1890s, it was used as something of an impromptu dance hall, where locals could waltz the night away, to the tunes of a band. Suitable lubrication came in the form of an assortment of alcoholic beverages.

Now it is Noa's domain, and she has truly made it her own. There's a living room, complete with a comfortable purple couch and armchair, strategically positioned in front of the television. Vines from house plants crisscross the walls. A swarm of paper birds hang from the ceiling on bits of string. There are all kinds of nicknacks and keepsakes. The walls are decorated with a diverse range of photos of the actor David Tennant portraying the demon Crowley in *Good Omens*; the robot Bender from *Futurama;* a watercolor of a French street cafe; and several CDs with anime characters printed on the front.

We confirm with Heather that we have Noa's express permission to be in her space without her being present. Her bedroom is more akin to a magical fairy grotto than a regular old bedroom, due mostly to the colorful outdoor mural which adorns the walls. The headboard of the bed is bedecked with flowers, among which are intertwined a set of blue holiday lights shaped like dragonflies.

"When Noa goes to bed at night, she locks the door," Heather says, "and it's in here that she feels an invisible somebody come into the room *through the locked door* and sit down on the edge of her bed. She'll sit up in bed to see who it is, and of course, there's never anybody there."

The teenager isn't freaked out by these strange goings-on. She was a little on edge at first, but soon grew accustomed to the weird nocturnal visits, and now barely gives them a second thought.

Equally strange is the apparition of a man that Heather has seen walking around on the third floor. This isn't a nebulous corner-of-the-eye sort of thing. She's adamant that the repeated encounters have been full-on, fully realized 3D ghost sightings, and she's able to describe the ghost to me. He's middle aged (she estimates early forties), about six feet high, and of slender build. The man wears charcoal grey trousers that are tailored formally; a plain white shirt, open at the neck; the entire ensemble seems to date back to the 1920s or 1930s in Heather's estimation.

"He's got mousey colored hair," she recalls, "which is cut short, going grey at the temples, with a slight wave to it. There's a short, neatly trimmed beard. I've seen him in the parlor, where the old front door would have been, walking through the hallway and on up the stairs, heading up in this direction. I've also seen him moving in the opposite direction, as though retracing his steps."

She confirms that the man is as solid and distinct as I am, standing in front of her right here and now. He never speaks, makes eye contact, or reacts to her presence in any way.

"The first few times I ran into him were during the daytime, thankfully. I actually mistook him for a member of the film crew to begin with! His dress never made him stand out, and he was walking with purpose, so I never really questioned it. The light bulb only went on over my head when I saw him after dark, when the house was otherwise empty."

"Does he always act in the same predictable way?" I want to know.

"All but once. He walked from the hallway into the parlor. Arryn was in the kitchen. I was sitting on the couch with Noa. He stopped, turned, and then looked into the room. *He wasn't looking at us.* Didn't acknowledge our present at all. He just goes on about his business."

She shrugs.

"It sounds very residual to me," I tell her. My companions nod. There's no indication of intelligence being present, based on what Heather has just told us. This sounds more like a paranormal recording-type haunting.

"I *think* so," she says uncertainly, "but I don't know..."

There's a collective intake of breath and all eyes shift toward the head of the bed. I turn to look. The chain of blue dragonfly lights has just started flashing, something they don't usually do. It happened the instant I said that the haunting sounded residual.

A strange synchronicity, but I doubt whether it's paranormal. Probably coincidental. The timing is interesting, however, and I can't help but wonder if somebody is trying to tell us something.

"Maybe we're getting a little greeting," says Jim.

Heather has to dash away, as a customer has come to visit her store downstairs. Stephen takes me aside and in a low voice, tells me that he had a spirit encounter just a week ago with a slender, bearded male clad in grey slacks and a white shirt. If it's the same man — and the description does indeed fit — then this wouldn't be the first time that he's gotten advance contact with a spirit from a location that we were soon to investigate.

The lights have stopped flashing, maintaining a steady blue state. Heather had switched them on when we first walked into the bedroom, and they stayed constant. They remain that way now. Rob stands there in the doorway, just observing. After a few minutes pass, nothing has changed, and he's gotten bored.

We spread out and set about exploring the third floor. Suddenly, a piercing shriek echoes throughout the house. I recognize the telltale sound of a smoke detector going off. The alarm wails for thirty seconds and then goes quiet. I wonder what set it off. Once again, the timing seems serendipitous.

Arryn confirms that the fire alert system does sometimes go off like that, for no apparent reason. The alarm company has not been able to provide an explanation for why. Just one of those things...or something weirder?

"This is an incredible place," Rob observes quietly.

"It is," I agree, and I've got the feeling that we're not going to have a quiet time."

On this, at least, I will be proven absolutely correct.

Chapter Eight

Arryn's Adult Beverages - Carrie

C arrie

1. *1.5 oz Absolut Citron (yes it does have to be Absolut Citron, if you don't have it make a different drink)*

2. *0.25 oz Cointreau (in this case it works better than Grand Marnier)*
   (I use a little less Cointreau than the classic as to keep the sweetness down)

3. *1 oz Ocean Spray Cranberry Cocktail Original (do not use anything lite or low sugar as it'll leave a weird aftertaste)*

4. *0.25 oz fresh squeezed lime juice (my only deviation from the classic is to add a small pinch of Maldon salt to the fresh lime juice so it dissolves in)*

5. *Add everything to a big metal shaker with lots of ice*

6. Shake like crazy thinking about which Sex & The City character you are

7. Once you've realized you're more Stanford than Samantha, strain into a chilled 90s style martini glass

8. Garnish with a lemon twist (try to get under ripe lemons so the skin is firm, and you can peel off a thin strip with little to no pith)

9. Drink with an air of superiority for bringing a classic back

H loves this drink, when the first S&TC movie opened, I made a big flask to sneak into the cinema when we went to see it (oh and we got so drunk we went to see the first Scooby-Doo live action movie straight afterwards!

....it was better).

Chapter Nine

Reaching Out

"From the very first moment I stepped foot in this house, I was aware that there were people here," Heather contemplates, referring to the resident ghosts. "I'd even go so far as to say that we're *crowded* at this point. I think a lot of that goes along with me bringing in so many objects for resale."

She's referring to her thriving personal business, dealing in antiques, curios and oddities. Who knows what attachments any one of them might have?

The Blumbergs — at least, those family members who *believe* in ghosts — are very welcoming, taking the view that the spirits were here long before they arrived; it's still their home. They have a prior claim on it. (Even if they aren't going to help out with the mortgage payments).

We make our way to the second floor. Heather casually mentions that several people have reported seeing the apparitions of two children in this part of the house. Some of the locals claim to have seen the faces of children in the windows of the house from the outside, though if this is the case, their identities remain unclear.

None of my sensitive teammates is picking up on that kind of energy. They'll let us know if that happens to change.

"How long was this house a functioning funeral home?" I want to know.

"Since 1913." That's more than a century of service to the community. Impressive. "Ambulances were also based here in the 1920s."

That ought to make fellow paramedic Jim and I feel at home. Heather thinks it's a conflict of interest, but historically speaking, there was a link between the funerary and fledgling pre-hospital services for many years. Not for nothing were so many early ambulances hearses. Morticians and funeral directors often wore the extra hat of running ambulance operations in addition to fulfilling their more traditional duties.

The master bedroom is a masterpiece of design, all black and gold with a huge gold star adorning the ceiling above the bed. The star took three weeks for Heather to cut out by hand.

Taking it all in for a moment, it feels like we're standing in the bedroom of a James Bond villain. The ensuite bathroom is one of the biggest I've ever seen. Satan is taking advantage of the cold tiles by stretching out and using them to cool his belly. Smart boy.

Hmmmf, Satan huffs, giving his tail a desultory wag and smacking the tile with an echoing crack like a gunshot.

Sticking with the Bond theme, this room has been done out in what looks like white and grey marble; at the touch of a button, a mirror rises up out of the countertop behind the sink.

Oh, and did I mention that it's also the only bathroom I've ever seen with an integrated wine rack?

There are even gold shower heads. I snap a picture and tell Heather I'm going to post it on Instagram, then tell people I'm investigating at Trump Tower. She clutches at her chest as if mortally wounded.

"Oh wow," Heather shakes her head, feigning outrage and hurt. "To think I quite liked him up until now..."

Stephen makes himself comfy in the bathroom.

Pulling aside the curtain, I look out of the window and see the swimming pool. My mind flashes back to the TV show, in which the pool was filled with all kinds of nasty flotsam and jetsam. It looks significantly cleaner now, thanks to a lot of hard work.

"The things we pulled out of there were absolutely horrific," she recalls. Now, you could actually take a dip in there and not feel the need to take a shower or ten afterward.

There's also one of the biggest closets I've ever seen. Poking my head inside, I'm astonished to see that it just goes back and back...presumably all the way to Narnia.

"Hey, everyone, there's a talking lion back here!" There's probably also a witch and some awful Turkish Delight.

Some parts of the house still need work. One of those rooms is a cluttered bedroom which is currently not serving any purpose beyond junk storage. There are several large and very ugly brown stains on the carpet, which I'm determined to steer well clear of. Bits of furniture are scattered around. There's also a couch. Light comes in via three tall windows. Still, despite all this, it clearly has a lot of potential, and I can only imagine the transformation this room will have undergone by the time this adventure is over and the book finally comes out.

"This is the room in which the hanging took place," Heather says, her voice solemn. I commit that to memory. The circumstances surrounding that death are unclear, and while details don't appear in any newspaper reports, several Dresdenites have confirmed that it did indeed take place. This room was formerly used for viewings of dead bodies. It is one of the few rooms which is fitted with a lock.

We're down on the ground floor now, in the parlor (aka the Pink Room) and my inner nerd is impressed to see props from the TV shows *Chucky* and *Star Trek: Discovery*. As I'm admiring the latter, a carved *objet d'art* belonging to an alien character, an enigmatic figure drifts through the room.

It's Raff.

He says hello, and then he's gone, disappearing downstairs into his lair. Hopefully he'll be joining us later.

Arryn is done with work for the day, so we get a chance to peek inside his office at the front of the house. This part of the structure isn't original. It is part of an extension that was added in the mid-1990s, overlooking the confluence of two streets.

Next comes the basement. There are two bedrooms — one for Raff, the other for his best friend and business partner, Doc. There's also a spacious and well-appointed gym. The showroom for Heather's store is also down here. Appropriately, it was once the casket showroom for potential customers. Now it's full of a diverse range of artifacts, at least one of which will be coming home with me. Arryn tags along with us. We meet Doc, who proves to be friendly and obligingly lets us take a look at his room.

Finally, we come to the jewel in the crown: the Speakeasy. The television cameras really didn't do it justice. Red velvet drapes adorn one wall, fronted by a glowing neon sign which declares: *Psychic Tarot Card Reader $10*. Off to the right is the infamous coffin bar, fully stocked with practically any liquor you'd care to name, and a few I've never even heard of. Stephen catches sight of it and begins to make very inappropriate sex noises to express his appreciation.

A record player and rows of vinyl records augment the brick wall to the right of that, and then we come to the cigar lounge. The entire room is bathed in crimson light, giving it a decidedly unearthly feel.

"This was the embalming room," Heather reminds us. There were originally floor to ceiling medical cabinets in here, which we've since ripped out. Our washing machine and tumble drier were in here when we moved in."

It's also, as we'll find out very soon, one of the most paranormally active parts of the house...if not the epicenter of the haunting.

"...and that's our tour," Heather says with a flourish. We're all boggled by not just the sheer amount of square footage we have to cover, but also by just how gorgeous the house is. It's clearly a labor of love, and one that will never be finished. Much like the process of painting a ship, where you start at the front, work your way to the back, and then start the whole thing over again, the funeral home will be a constant work in progress. Heather is clearly restless, her mind constantly dreaming up new projects and scenarios for this magnificent blank canvas. Her mind sees all of the untapped potential. It will never be done.

I can't help but wonder what the ghosts make of that. Does the constant state of redesign, construction and decoration annoy them? Does it anger them? Perhaps the opposite might be true. Maybe they find it stimulating, the equivalent of an ongoing soap opera or live action TV design show.

There's only one way to find out.

We need to reach out and ask them.

A constant thread running through our investigation of the Blumberg residence is: *why?*

More specifically, why would a place like this be haunted? The answer seems ridiculously obvious. We justifiably equate this property with death, and we equate death with ghosts. *Et voila.*

That's a simplistic answer — which doesn't mean it isn't also the correct one — but there might be other explanations at work here too. Heather has her own beliefs and shares them with us after the tour is over.

"It's all about energy. We are made up of energy, and I believe that we leave some of it behind in virtually everything that we do. They're driven by emotions, both good and bad. This house, I think, is full of good. Funerals bring sadness, because someone you love has left you...but at the same time, you're there celebrating the life of somebody you loved. That's why this house feels light and good to me."

"...and nurturing," interjects Stephen. Heather nods in agreement.

"I've been in other places which felt completely different. There, the sensation was one of being threatened."

A case in point is a basement apartment that Heather and Arryn once resided at in London's trendy Notting Hill district. Although Arryn remains unruffled by it all, hiding his thoughts behind an inscrutable half smile, heather reveals that she found the energies there to be dark and intimidating...so much so that, whenever she went to the restroom at night, she first turned on all the lights. An invisible somebody would sit down on the bed — exactly what happens to Noa in her room on the third floor.

More disconcerting still was the night on which Heather was jolted awake from her sleep by unseen hands which grabbed her roughly. "*He* wouldn't believe me—" she jabs a thumb in Arryn's direction "— until the next day, when a load of bruises came up on the side of my arm."

Arryn remains diplomatically silent.

What Heather's describing sounds like an aggressive haunting, and doubtless if her story was featured on one of the many paranormal "reality" TV or YouTube shows, it would be portrayed as being malevolent and dangerous. Indeed, Heather certainly felt threatened. Yet it's also possible that this was simply a frustrated human spirit that was trying to make its presence known in the only way it knew how. It's my belief that many such hauntings have been misinterpreted as being dark and, I hate to say, supposedly demonic.

Heather has made her beliefs very clear. I'm equally fascinated to learn about Arryn's.

"On the TV show, you came across as the humorous but polite skeptic. Living here day in, day out, with no cameras on you, do you still retain that attitude, or do you believe something different?"

"Most of the time, that's still my approach, but there have been some odd things which have made me question them."

"For example?"

"Well, my office used to be the room upstairs at the top of the stairs. The one in which the hanging took place. I was working away in there one lunchtime and heard somebody shout '*Hello.*' It's a big building, right? So, it could be anybody. Perhaps somebody came in from the street, but I thought it more likely to have been Heather or Becky [a friend of the family whom we'll meet later]."

That makes sense. The voice was female and, if Arryn's memory is accurate, belonged to a woman in her forties or fifties.

"I wasn't really paying a lot of attention to it," he goes on. "I shouted back an acknowledgment. *Hello!* No response. So, I got up from my desk and went to the top of the stairs. Shouted hello again. Still no response. I called Heather on the phone. It turns out that she was out of the house at the time, so I checked the house. There was no sign of Becky or anybody else. Raff and Noa weren't home either."

To this day, Arryn has no explanation. It's possible that he simply imagined it, but he isn't the only person to have heard a female voice calling out inside the house, and I suspect he won't be the last.

He's also seen shadows moving inside the house. Notably, this has happened inside internal rooms with no windows on the outside world. This makes it less likely that the movement of tree branches or cars going past outside could be responsible.

Then there's the coffee cup.

"Yeah," Arryn admits, "that *was* weird."

Heather had set a coffee cup down on the living room table. Apropos of nothing, while an astonished Heather and Arryn looked on, the cup slid roughly one foot to fourteen inches across the glass tabletop before landing on the floor. Nobody had been anywhere near it at the time. Fortunately, the cup was empty.

Once again, as with so much which takes place within the walls of this house, there was no obvious explanation — apart from the paranormal.

Before getting down to the business of investigating, there's a bunch of growling stomachs to be appeased. For snacks, Heather recommends the Union Block Bakery, which is just a short walk away from the house. Apparently, it has cakes, cookies, and sweet treats to die for. Leaving Heather and Arryn to their own devices for a while, we stroll in that direction, getting a sense for Dresden as we go. There's an assortment of homes and small businesses of the kind you might find in almost any town.

What follows once we arrive at the Union Block Bakery might best be described as a glucose blizzard. Sugar comes our way in the form of donuts, teacakes, buns, and in my case (being a non-coffee drinker) a tall cup of hot chocolate.

Chatting excitedly about the house, the Blumbergs, and the adventure on which we're now embarking in earnest, we each ingest enough sugary calories to gain a pound in weight apiece. Before we leave, we pick up a to go box for our hosts as a small token of our appreciation.

It's close to three o'clock by the time we get back. Once again, there's a tail-wagging, barking and drooling welcoming committee. In addition to Satan, Beans and Pork, Noa is home from school. (In the interests of clarity, I must point out that she was neither wagging, barking, nor drooling herself.) There are more introductions, and we begin unloading our equipment cases from the car. Monkey, as she prefers to be called, shows a keen interest in the array of gadgets, devices and esoterica we've brought in from the States.

There are Rem-Pods, EMF meters, digital voice recorders and analog tape recorders. At the less technological end of the spectrum, there are Ouija boards and dowsing rods. Then there are the batteries...hundreds of dollars' worth of batteries, all of them either rechargeable (these go onto chargers straight away) or factory fresh, fully charged Duracells. AAs, AAAs, 9 volts, and more. Unexplained battery drains are a common occurrence in haunted locations, and we don't want to get caught without the proper type.

"The dogs are exhausted," Heather tells Noa, explaining that they've followed us all around the house today, and in the process have been relentlessly snuggled.

"Were they good?" Noa asks.

"Meh," Heather rocks her hand from side to side.

Now that the youngest Blumberg is home, we can obtain permission to investigate Noa's living space from her directly. We make our way up to the third floor, each of us carrying an armful of equipment. All three of the dogs elect to join us, padding up the staircase at our heels. The team spreads out, dividing ourselves up between Noa's bedroom, the couch in her living room, and the landing at the top of the stairs.

Rem-Pods and Parascopes are deployed. The Rem-Pod generates an electromagnetic field which, when disturbed by either a physical intruder or radio waves, will flash a sequence of lights and generate an annoying screeching noise. The Parascope measures positive and negative fields of static electricity. It's essentially a disc with sixteen transparent rods sticking out of the sides, like the spokes in a bicycle wheel. Each of those sixteen indicates a different level of voltage has been detected by one or more of the device's four antennae. The Parascope is good for detecting those static energy changes. For paranormal investigators, the key question therefore becomes: do ghosts give off static electricity, or are they connected with it in some way? I don't have a lot of experience with this particular gadget, and I'm fascinated to give it a shot.

Our investigators have dispersed themselves at relatively even intervals across the third floor. I'm making full use of the very comfortable couch. Everyone is keeping a close eye out for the apparition of the man in period clothing that Heather has repeatedly seen up here.

There's a tap-tap-tapping sound which takes us a moment to place. It's the sound of rain spattering against the windows and the roof, one of those early afternoon showers which Dresden often gets at around this time. It doesn't bother the dogs, who each finds his own bit of comfortable carpet or floorboard and collapses in an ungainly heap. I keep an eye on them too, reasoning that they're the best type of organic ghost detector I could ever wish for.

Moving away from the biological and into the realm of the technological, I'm giving a new paranormal app a try. Some fellow investigators have told me they've had promising results with it. According to the app's designers, it uses sensors installed in your phone or tablet to read changes in energy levels around the device. If I have it right, those readings are then converted into words using a process of which I have absolutely no understanding, which an artificial intelligence subsequently uses to construct images on the screen. It's a fascinating concept and having given it a try already at another haunted location, I was sufficiently intrigued by the results that I want to use it again here in Dresden.

I'm a little wary because I don't know exactly what's going on under the hood with this particular app. It needs an Internet connection, and access to my tablet's camera and microphone in order to do what it does. The suspicious part of me wonders whether it might be zeroing in on my location, or listening to words that are spoken around the mic and using them as inputs. For example, if my GPS pinged me at an old hospital, or I said the word "hospital" two or three times in a relatively short time span, would the app be aware of that and begin tailoring its images toward a medical theme?

On the other hand, I previously had an experience with it that I simply cannot explain. It took place at Tinker's Swiss Cottage in Illinois. I was trying the app out, and explained as best I could to two of my colleagues how it was supposed to work. They both attempted to psychically influence the next image which appeared on the screen. It's important for me to add that neither of these gentleman professes themselves to be sensitive in the slightest. In fact, they're very much the opposite. Hard-charging, bull-headed good guys who fall under the banner of technical investigators, using technological methods while researching claims of the paranormal. It would be difficult to find two more traditional, down-to-Earth people on which to test the app.

At first, there was no luck. But then, an image popped up on my iPad's screen which startled one of them. He had been thinking of a pirate ship, putting as much mental force into it as he possibly could. The picture on the screen was that of an old-fashioned sailing ship...one with a distinctly pirate-like vibe.

There was nothing about the location on the map which suggested ships, rivers, or oceans, let alone pirates. Neither did any of us say anything relating to those subjects. What are the odds that the app could simply have guessed something that specific? Pretty small, to say the least.

So, with the jury still out, I'm intrigued to see what it comes up with here in Dresden. I leave the app running throughout our investigation.

Meanwhile, Jill has started out with a basic, interesting method of attempted spirit communication: a pendulum. This dangles on a small chain from her hand and rotates in one direction for yes, and the opposite for no. Skeptics dismiss pendulum activity as being nothing more than micro-muscular tremors, the sort of tremulousness that all of us, even the steadiest, experience on an everyday basis. It's also claimed that the pendulum is being driven by the power of suggestion. In some instances, I have no doubt that this is the case. I'm not so sure that it applies one hundred percent of the time though, and I settle in to watch Jill work, while Jim feeds her questions.

She asks about the number of spirits that are present in the room with us at the present time, going up to "four" before getting an affirmative response from the pendulum. I wonder aloud if one of them is the male apparition that Heather has seen. The answer comes back as a rapid yes.

"Is he here all the time?" Jill enquires. *Yes.*

"Did he live here when he was in the physical body?" *No.*

Nor was his funeral held in this house, which I find to be interesting. Bias is a very real thing, and it's all too easy for us to assume that the spirits we might encounter in this house are related to its history as a funeral home. That's a likely explanation, but only one of several potential answers.

In fact, if Jill's pendulum is correct, he's here to deliver a message to somebody — somebody he knew back in his lifetime, a former resident of this home. *That* person did not die in the house either, but their funeral took place here.

"Is he revealing himself to Heather intentionally," Jill goes on, "deliberately allowing her to see him?"

That's a very enthusiastic yes, taking the pendulum a moment or two to settle back into its neutral position again. He believes that Heather can help him in some way. He's currently away from the house, however, leading us to wonder where exactly he might be and what his message for Heather is.

Shifting gears, Jill asks about the spirit of a young female that has been reported by some to haunt the house. The pendulum confirms that she is indeed an active spirit here, having died in the house many years ago. She is kept company by at least one other female spirit.

Jill asks whether the fire alarm incident was accidental. "That's a pretty big no," Jim observes, watching the pendulum twist sharply about its axis.

"Did one of the spirits here set that off?" *Yes*, the pendulum responds.

"What about the lights in Noa's bedroom?" Stephen interjects, referring to the dragonflies. "Was a spirit playing with those earlier?"

Again, the answer — if an answer it truly is — seems to be yes.

From Noa's living room, there comes a clattering sound. Rob, who is all alone in there, sitting on the couch and minding his own business, looks up, trying to locate the source.

"What fell?" I ask.

He tracks it down fairly quickly. Two of the CDs pinned to the wall by the window have fallen onto the carpet. Nobody was near them at the time. Nobody was walking around, potentially creating vibrations. All was still and quiet as we focused on Jill and her pendulum. Neither did any of our sensors go off.

"Did someone knock those off the wall in an attempt to get some attention?" she wants to know. The answer is an unequivocal yes. "Can you do that again?"

There's no response.

My tablet pings. It's an AI-drawn image...of two young females, drawn from behind, standing in front of some tall windows.

"Is that a representation of you?" Jill asks, indicating the screen with a nod of her head. The pendulum says that it is. Interesting. It could simply be a coincidence. It could be that the software is listening to us — I can't say for sure either way. But it could also be the case that it's doing exactly what it's claimed it does, offering the spirits some bizarre and unorthodox method for communicating with us.

Now the pendulum tells Jill that the spirit of a man is keeping Rob company in Noa's living room. When he hears this, Rob's ever-present hangdog expression doesn't change. He just casts a look around the room and settles back into his ghost watch, keeping an eye on the instruments and waiting for something else to happen.

Stephen and Jill, meanwhile, are in the process of trying to identify the *next* communicator who seems to have jumped in and hijacked the pendulum. This claims to be a man whose name begins with the letter C; a man who haunts the property because his funeral took place here. By a process of throwing out as many male names beginning with C, they finally get a hit on a specific name. If the pendulum is to be believed, then he's a relatively recent addition to the ghost family of the house. As an author, I'll say no more about him, simply because a very specific name was given and there may be family members still living in the vicinity.

A loud rumble of thunder crashes off in the distance. It's a dark and stormy…well, afternoon, but that doesn't make it feel any less fitting for both the occasion and the location.

Jill enquires whether there are any spirits hanging out downstairs with the Blumbergs, two of whom are watching a little afternoon TV. The affirmative answer brings to mind an image of Noa and Heather lounging on the massive couch, perhaps with a dog or two between them, and a small crowd of unseen spirits gathered around them, checking out whatever entertainment show the ladies have chosen to watch.

A cold breeze snakes through the room, rippling one of the wall hangings. Our sensor equipment picks up the temperature drop. It's nothing paranormal. A tendril from the thunderstorm has made its way into the house. Rob confirms it by identifying a small gap in the windowpane.

Jill closes down the pendulum, ending the communication session. It's good practice, in both the life and the afterlife, to close down any door that you might open...just in case.

Next up, Jim elects to give his dowsing rods a shot. Unfortunately, they refuse to play ball.

"I think they've all gone downstairs," Stephen says, meaning the spirits. "We should probably follow them. I feel like taking a break anyway."

There's no faulting his logic, so that's exactly what we do.

Once we reach the living room, I let Noa know about the CDs falling. "That's happened before," she tells us, completely unfazed. That makes me lean toward it being a perfectly natural occurrence, though I can also recall the pendulum telling Jill that spirits were responsible for dropping them onto the carpet.

We chill out in the living room for a little while, shooting the breeze with Noa and Heather. After a while, we decide to go back up, this time carrying a Ouija board. Despite the bias many people have toward them, I've always found such boards to be tools like any other. The hair-raising, spine-chilling mystique which centers upon them really began with the release of the book and movie adaptions of *The Exorcist* during the early 1970s. Prior to that, many people believed the Ouija and its derivatives to be nothing more than harmless fun. It lacked the association with demons and darkness that many people find so terrifying today.

We open the board up with the usual protective precautions, stipulating that we're only willing to communicate with good, truthful spirits, rather than any that are deceptive and negative in nature.

Things start promisingly when the board spells out that we're talking with a 75-year-old woman.

"What year were you born?" Jim asks, his fingertip on the planchette along with Stephen and Jill. *1936* is the answer. "Was your funeral held here, in this funeral home?"

Again, the answer is *yes*. This might be a spirit, or it could also be the subconscious of one of the participants. Either way, it's a fascinating beginning.

"Did you have any children?"

The planchette slides slowly across the board, coming to a stop above number *Three*.

"How many of them were boys?"

The planchette hovers over the number *One*.

"That means you had two girls, right?" Jim asks.

Yes, responds the board.

Jim asks whether she was born in Dresden and is told that she was. Further, the invisible communicator claims that her headstone can be found in the local cemetery. Intriguing! All we need now is a name.

Unfortunately, it isn't forthcoming. The board clams up. At first, it seems that the lack of movement means that there's nobody around who's either willing or able to talk to us. Then, the planchette starts moving again, announcing the arrival of a new communicator. Their name comes across quickly and fluidly: *Stephen.*

Stephen's next message seems like gobbledygook at first. The board darts from one letter to the next in rapid succession, tracing the following path: RUAWITCH. We're not always quick on the uptake. It takes a moment for us to realize that it seems to be asking: "Are you a witch?"

"No," our own Stephen declares emphatically.

"Stephen, are you from Dresden?" Jim asks.

"I am," the board spells out.

"Can we ask how old you are?"

35 is the answer.

"What year were you born?"

1857.

"Is there anything else you'd like to communicate with us?"

Die.

Well, *there's* a thing...

It would be easy to spin this as a threat, but instead Jim asks for clarification. "Are you saying that you died?"

The planchette slides across to the word *Yes*.

Next comes RUDIE? It could be a name, but more likely, it's an attempt to ask whether we're dead. It's entirely possible that our communicator is semi-literate; alternatively, they're doing the Ouija board equivalent of text-speak, using shorthand in order to tap out the fewest possible characters with which to answer.

"Did you have an education?" our Stephen asks politely. His namesake confirms that yes, he did.

Jim asks whether Stephen is from Canada originally and is told *No*; nor is invisi-Stephen from the US. He claims to be European — more specifically, Germany.

"Just confirming that you're from Germany?" Jim says. *Ja* is the immediate reply. Jim responds with a sentence in German, which I learn later says "My family comes from Germany...do you understand?"

The planchette moves directly to *Yes*.

What follows is a conversation in German which attempts to locate Stephen's hometown. It ends, once again, with *IDIE*.

Energy is running low. The group is getting tired. We say goodbye to Stephen — or perhaps that should be *auf wiedersehn* — and then close down the board, shutting the door politely but firmly on our new Germanic friend.

Chapter Ten

Arryn's Adult Beverages - Never Sleep Again

N*ever Sleep Again*
12 oz Belvedere Vodka

2. *0.5 oz Kahlua Coffee Liquor*

3. *0.25 oz Frangelico Hazelnut Liqueur (this is what makes my take on an espresso martini special)*

4. *2-3 drops Angostura bitters (if you can find a cocoa or coffee bitters use that)*

5. *0.75 oz chilled coffee (we make French press espresso most mornings and there is always some left over, I add a heaped*

teaspoon of Nescafe Rich Intense instant coffee to about half a cup of leftover coffee to create a super strong mixer...a chilled Nespresso shot of something strong works as well, but I prefer the intensity of the Nescafe as it adds flavour without liquid)

6. *Put all the ingredients into a shaker full of ice and go.*

7. *Shake until everything is icy icy cold and you've created a bit of dilution from the ice*

8. *Strain into a chilled dinner coffee mug (you know the type that is heavy, white with a green or red stripe, always spills a bit when you take a sip)*

9. *Enjoy on your next Zoom call as you explain you like a decaf for the flavor towards the end of the day...*

Chapter Eleven

"Come to Us."

A fter another quick break, there's some discussion about where to investigate next. The constant drumming of the rain on the outside of the house means that any audio we record aboveground will almost certainly be contaminated.

"I'd like to spend some time down in the Speakeasy," Stephen says.

"Maybe throw down some recorders and see what happens," adds Rob.

"Good idea," Jim agrees.

Rob taps the side of his head. "Not just a hat rack."

The Speakeasy it is. We make ourselves comfortable in the red underground chamber. It has an easy, relaxing atmosphere. Despite its prior history as an embalming room, it feels like somewhere I could lie down and take a nap if I needed to.

You can barely hear the rain down here, which makes it absolutely perfect for our purposes. Stephen plays some light jazz music, to help set the mood. The strains of trumpets, trombones and saxophones are the backdrop to the following hour of our lives.

We sit there quietly, soaking it all in and just allowing our recorders to run.

Ever since our conversation with the other Stephen via the Ouija board, Jill has been working on some background research. She's located a Stephen who immigrated from Germany to Ontario and was born in 1857. That could be our guy, except for the fact that Ontario is a big province, and there's no guarantee that it's the same Stephen. Still, it's a piece of good initial detective work on our part, and she's determined to stick with it and see what else she can dig up.

"We have a visitor," our Stephen announces, sitting up straighter in his chair and glancing toward the door. He's in full-on psychic mode now. "Come on in and talk with us."

All eyes turn expectantly in that direction. There's nothing to be seen in the wan red glow. Nothing stirs, and so we wait...

...and wait...

...and wait.

We chat politely, in low quiet voices. I have a digital voice recorder running on top of the small table in the center of the room. Although we won't know it until the evidence review phase, it picks up a very bizarre EVP. It is an indisputable fact that the only people present in the house are adults, or close to being adults (the youngest being Noa, who is still upstairs with her mother). On playback, shortly after Stephen;'s announcement that we are being visited, what is clearly a child's voice starts speaking over the hushed conversation he and I are having. This is a Class B EVP, a step down from Class A, which are the best. It's definitely a voice, there's no debating that. The first part of the sentence, which is spoken in a high-pitched tone, could not be coming from an adult. At the end of what sound like three or four unintelligible words comes the word: *Daddy.*

After cleaning the EVP up with audio enhancement software, I put the sound clip out there and invited people to give their opinion on what it might say. As with any EVP, different people hear different things, and have their own unique interpretations of what's being said.

Heather Blumberg hears "I'm there beside Daddy." (I have it on good authority that this freaked Arryn out significantly!)

Social media and Patreon supporter responses included hearing phrases such as: *that's/it's mine; it is time — it's Daddy; thank you; 6...5...65; this is the time; this is my room; get outta here...* and various others. All this goes to prove that hearing an anomalous EVP is one thing, but interpreting it is another thing entirely; an almost completely subjective experience, which few people hearing the same thing until somebody points out what *they* hear, thereby introducing an element of bias into the mix.

None of which detracts from the fact that there's a child's voice talking to us in the Speakeasy for which we have absolutely no non-paranormal explanation. None of us hear anything unusual at the time. None of us react. If it weren't for Stephen sensing the arrival of a visitor, we'd simply be sitting there in blissful ignorance.

Could this be one of the several children which visiting sensitives have claimed haunt the old funeral home? It certainly seems that way.

I'm tempted to keep a running tally on the number of EVPs we each record during the trip, but I suspect that Rob, who isn't the most competitive guy when it comes to investigating, won't be thrilled if we start keeping score, so instead we have a tally ban for the duration of the case. I mentally label it "Rob's tally ban."

There's a chime from my tablet. The image-generating app has generated a picture of two people in white gowns or aprons, their chests covered in bright red blood splatter. One possible interpretation might be that they're involved in embalming. Another would be some kind of surgical procedure. There's definitely a "we're working on the innards of a prone body" vibe to the picture. I save it to my photo gallery, mentally filing it away as "interesting but unproven."

Equally interesting is the next image, which shows four faceless people in chairs gathering around a table. It's interesting because down here in the Speakeasy, there are four of us — Rob, Stephen, Jill, and I — gathered around a table. (Stephen and Jim are sitting off to the side). Art really does seem to be mirroring life. There's no way the app could tell, even with access to my camera, how many of us are seated around it.

Hmmm.

Color me intrigued.

My phone pings. It's a text from fellow investigator Brad. He and Tim have just checked into what he colorfully describes as "a serial killer motel." Stephen and Jim are also staying there, so hopefully they all survive the night. Based on fact that there's "do not enter" yellow tape crisscrossing a broken window, I don't know how much of an exaggeration that is. All being well, the intrepid duo will be joining us shortly, and our core team will be complete.

Our next investigative technique will be an Estes Session, carried out right here in the embalming room/Speakeasy. We're using an SB-7 spirit box, professional quality headphones, and an eye mask to induce a state of light sensory deprivation for our first volunteer listener, which is going to be Jim. While he's getting set up, the app pings again with a new image. It depicts an adult male with glasses, and hair that's not dissimilar to my own, alongside another man who has both his eyes and his ears covered up. Considering what we're about to do, that seems like one hell of a coincidence — if a coincidence it truly is.

Jim is now fully in Estes mode, unable to see, and only able to hear the output from the spirit box as it scans its way through multiple radio frequencies. His breathing falls into a slower, deeper rhythm. The rest of us invite anybody who wants to communicate with us to start talking.

It's a quiet session, and we halfway expect it to be. This deep in the building, we're not getting the greatest radio reception. Still, we each take turns asking questions, trying to make contact with whoever might be around. The best we get is a chorus of gurgling stomachs, remind all of us that we've only eaten sugary treats today, and no substantial whole food.

It is, if you'll pardon the expression, as quiet as the grave. Jim's breathing is now sufficiently deep that we're wondering whether he's fallen asleep. It turns out he hasn't. A tap on the shoulder brings him out. It's looking as though the Estes Method is going to be a bust down here — not for the lack of spirits, I suspect, but because of the weak radio reception.

However, Stephen is unwilling to give up quite so easily. He wants to give it a try himself. Rather than here in the Speakeasy, he walks through the glass door into the Cigar Lounge and takes a seat in a beautifully upholstered barber's chair. It's surreal to think that just a few years ago, this space was used for the embalming of numerous human bodies.

Settling himself in the seat, blindfold on and headphones in place, Stephen is soon fully under. The SB-7 rests in his lap. He fiddles blindly with the sweep rate until he finds a setting that he likes. Just to be sure, we also change the battery in the spirit box. It should already have been well-charged, but a change can't hurt.

I head upstairs to help put in an order for pizza.

This session is night and day different to the first one. Jim is asking the questions this time out. Stephen opens with *"Up."*

"Richard just went upstairs," Jim acknowledges.

"Hello."

"Hello! My name is Jim. What's your name?"

A pause, then: *"Asgard."*

"Asgard? Are we talking to someone from Norway?"

"Yeah."

"Do you know where you are today?"

"Afraid not," Stephen replies.

"Are you a man or a woman?"

"Woman."

"Well, it's nice to meet you."

"Hi. Hi."

"Hi!" Jim says.

"What is that?"

"It's a device used for taking pictures. Photographs," Jim explains. "May I ask your name?"

"Linda."

"How old are you, Linda?" There's no answer. "I know it's not polite for a man to ask a lady that question, but..."

"Eighty," is the seemingly reluctant reply.

"Did you live in Dresden, Linda?"

"Some."

Jim follows up by asking Linda what year she was born. The answer — *"purple"* — makes no sense. "Are you the only person here who wants to talk to us?"

"No." This is followed by: *"Cold."*

"It is cold outside," agrees Jim.

"Or are you telling us that *you're* cold?" Rob enquires.

When there's no reply, Jill asks whether Linda was married.

"In here," Stephen responds.

"What is your husband's name?"

"Wake up. Dead. 65."

"Did you die at 65?"

"We did."

That makes no sense. How can Linda be 80, and yet have died at the age of 65...unless, that is, she died 15 years ago and is still counting off the years as they pass?

"Who was with you?" interjects Jill.

"I am."

"Linda, is there another person with you?"

"Yeah."

"May I ask their name please?" Jim remains formal and polite.

"Son." Next comes: *"Embalmed."*

Jim asks Linda whether her funeral was held here in the house. *"Aye,"* is the response. *"Attachment."*

Now there's an interesting word. It comes again ten seconds later. In paranormal circles, that may mean somebody has a spirit entity attached to them. Just as we're all wondering who Linda is referring to, Stephen says *"Rob."*

Our own Rob is suddenly getting a lot of side eye.

"Dark man," Stephen adds, his tone flat and devoid of emotion or emphasis. Things have taken a turn for the sinister. Then they get a bit nautical, with *"boat"* and *"breakers."*

"Come. To. Us."

That sends a chill down our collective spines. Partly it's the choice of words; partly it's the monotone manner of delivery.

"Come to you where?"

"Egypt."

Jill perks up. She's recently returned from a trip to Egypt. Could there be a connection...or are we reaching?

"Does someone have an attachment?" Jim asks, trying to clarify.

"No," Stephen shakes his head. Then: "Kids..."

At the time, we don't recognize the significance of the word *kids*. However, when viewed in light of the child-like EVP that we unknowingly recorded half an hour ago, it begins to look decidedly more relevant.

"Drown," comes next. It's followed by repeated requests for help.

After this, the session degenerates into a string of mostly non-sensical non-sequiturs. I check my watch. Stephen has been under for close to half an hour. It's time to bring him out. Jill shakes him gently. He slips off the headphones and sets them aside, then removes the blindfold.

"Three distinct voices kept coming through," he explains, blinking. "Two males and a female; she was in distress. The two males were in conversation with one another."

Some of it — primarily the conversation with Linda — seemed meaningful. The remainder was gibberish. I think it's a good idea for us to call it when we did. Such rapid degeneration in the quality of communication suggests that somebody (either the speakers, the listener, or both) is getting tired.

Besides, a chime from the doorbell announces the arrival of not just pizza, but also Brad and Tim. Introductions happen first, followed by a dive into several deep-dish delights which have us all salivating. Satan, Beans, and Pork eye us hungrily with the look of a salivating wolf pack that's sizing up its chances of tearing everyone apart in order to get to the pizza.

We shouldn't give them human food, but I'd be gravely disappointed in any member of my team who didn't at least try to sneak the boys a tasty tidbit or two from their own plates. This is something I hear, rather than see, as our group conversation is regularly interrupted by the sound of jaws snapping shut like a steel trap on a bit of meat and crust.

We congregate in the kitchen and bring the two newcomers up to speed. There's an abbreviated tour of the house, just giving them the highlights. I'm surprised to see how late it's gotten, and I'm cognizant that the Blumbergs have put up with our intrusion gracefully all day. Now, it seems as though the right thing to do is to let them enjoy some quality family time without us.

It's an excited group of paranormal investigators that files out into the night. Jill and I are both staying at a hotel in nearby Chatham-Kent. Rob has gotten himself an AirBnB for the duration of our visit. Stephen, Jim, Tim and Brad have all gone for the same motel.

On the drive back, the car is full of excited chatter concerning the events of day one. We're in complete agreement that today was just the tip of the iceberg, and that the former funeral home has so much more to teach us.

Just how true that is, we have absolutely no idea. But we're about to find out.

Chapter Twelve

Arryn's Adult Beverages - Crescent City

C **rescent City**

1. *1 oz Wild Turkey 101 Rye (or another good rye whiskey, you can use a peaty Scotch or Irish whiskey for a nice variation)*

2. *A ¼ - ½ -bar spoon Lucid Absinthe (or another real absinthe)*

*Go carefully! Not only is the real stuff very, **very** strong but it has an overpowering flavor if you use too much*

(If you don't want to drink the absinthe, embracing your inner Hemingway in the process, you can use 1 oz of absinthe as a wash for you glass i.e. put the absinthe in your chilled rocks glass, swirl around and tip the liquid out)

3. *2-3 drops Peychaud's Bitters*

4. *A small pinch of brown sugar*

The classic version uses a full sugar cube, but I find it makes the drink too sweet and syrupy

5.   *Put all this in a glass cocktail mixer, crushing the sugar first with a muddler, then add lots of ice and stir until the drink is cold*

The key to enjoying the absinthe is the dilution i.e. adding water from melting ice

6.   *Strain into a chilled rocks glass over a fancy single large ice cube (square or round)*

If you prefer a more authentic drink, leave out the ice cube but personally I like the ongoing chill

7.   *Garnish with a lemon twist*

8.   *Drink carefully, these pack a punch*

Chapter Thirteen

Zoot Suits, Egypt, & Witches

The next morning dawns bright and clear in Chatham-Kent. Jill, Stephen and I take the rental car to pick up Rob, who has spent the night living in somebody's basement, and we meet Jim, Brad and Tim at a local cafe for breakfast and coffee. Then it's on to the nearest Tim Horton's for more coffee and other caffeinated beverages and snacks to see us through the day's shenanigans.

Jim has a prior commitment, so has to hit the road for home. After saying our goodbyes, the rest of us head for Dresden.

Once we arrive at the funeral home and get the inevitable doggy greeting out of the way (something we're in no rush to do) we catch up with Heather and learn that our activities of the day before seem to have stirred something up. Noa left for school around 7:30 this morning. About an hour later, the sound of footsteps could be clearly heard walking around her empty bedroom and living area. The entire third floor was deserted at the time.

None of us thinks it's a coincidence.

Neither was that the only disturbance. At 2:20am, first Arryn and then Heather were woken up from a deep sleep by the sound of a loud shout from somewhere within the house. It was followed two minutes later by two extremely loud bangs. When she and Arryn searched the house, nothing was out of place. The sound hadn't come from the dogs, all of whom were slumbering peacefully. So were Raff and Noa, neither of whom heard a thing.

Brad and Tim decide to make that their first stop. They're fresh to the house, and Noa's lair seems like a great place for them to get set up and start investigating.

Jill wants to investigate the hanging room, so we're going to focus on that first.

Raff and Doc will be downstairs. Heather's heading out for a few hours to do some shopping. Before doing so, she's switched off the heating and air, so there's one less source of mechanical contamination for us to contend with.

I accompany Stephen, Jill and Rob up to the second floor. We make our way to the hanging room, which is situated at the back of the house. The room is cluttered, still waiting for its makeover into something fabulous. All four of us take a seat on what furniture we can find, or pull up a bit of carpet, being careful to avoid the stained patches. After all, this is *not* a house you'd want to bring a black light into.

We all know that this has to be approached delicately. Suicide is a tragic thing, and the last thing any of us wants to do is to re-traumatize anybody who might still be here after the fact. Jill leads off with some gentle questioning, trying to make contact with any potential communicator. Our EVP recorders log everything for posterity.

Thud. Bang. Creak. We look up. There's noise contamination coming from up above us on the third floor, as Tim and Brad settle in to do their thing. It quickly becomes apparent that our two groups are too close together. Whatever we do will interfere with the audio data of the other group. Stephen suggests we relocate to the garage, another floor down, in order to put a buffer between our groups. It's a good idea.

This is Heather's store, full of curios and knickknacks. Everybody is quickly enraptured with the various bargains that are on display, many of them marked down far lower than they'd cost in the US. Jill breaks out her pendulum and watches it spin in seeming response to her questions. If this is genuine communication, and not simply ideomotor muscle tremors at work, then whoever she's interacting with claims to be attached to an object in this store...more specifically, a book.

Heather's store.

She uses the pendulum to guide her on a "getting warmer/colder" quest to identify the exact book in question. Jill moves through the aisles, turning left and right at the pendulum's behest. Unfortunately, the directions make no apparent sense...until she asks whether the book is located somewhere else in the house. She's told that yes, the book can in fact be found upstairs in the funeral home, not here in the garage/store.

While Jill pursues this line of enquiry, Rob moves to the lowest level of the shop and begins poking around, examining the various bargains in the hopes of finding something that appeals to him. He could happily spend hours going through them all.

Stephen asks questions while Jill holds the pendulum, which twirls and spins on a tiny chain. The communicator claims to be a 12-year-old girl who attended a funeral here in the house...the funeral of her own mother.

"Are you here because she's here?" Jill asks. There's no answer. "Are you looking for your mother."

Yes.

The pendulum says that the 12-year-old has been unable to find her mother, and now feels as if they're stuck here. Again, with the benefit of hindsight, I can't help but wonder whether this has anything to do with the child-like EVP we recorded in the Speakeasy the day before. It sounded very much like the voice of a little girl. Could there be a connection?

In an attempt to find out, the garage team conducts a burst EVP session. They start a recorder running and ask a few basic questions, giving ample opportunity between them for a response to be imprinted on the recording. Despite everybody's best efforts, it doesn't happen.

At the same time, Brad and Tim have been getting acquainted with the third floor. They're ensconced on the comfortable furniture in Noa's living area, and quickly get set up for an Estes Method session.

First to go under the hood is Brad. He sits forward on the couch, fingers loosely interlaced between his knees. Tim asks the questions, making notes as he goes along.

"I come," seems to herald the arrival of a communicator, who's speaking to Brad through the spirit box. I set down my tablet, making sure that its camera is pointing at a blank patch of wall. The AI app generates a picture of a bald man with eyes covered by some sort of black band. It looks eerily like Brad, and there's no way the app could know what he looks like or what he's doing.

The winds are picking up outside, making the windows rattle slightly in their frames. Although Brad is speaking words such as *"two fingers"* and *"center,"* none of it bears any obvious relevance to the situation at hand, or to the questions that Tim is asking. He forges ahead regardless, continuing to ask calm and concise questions. There's a smattering of names, such as Jeffrey and Susan, but when Tim asks whether those are the names of whoever is speaking to Brad, he's told: *"Not the same."*

Estes session in Noa's living space. L-R: Jill, Heather, Brad, Tim, Stephen.

Later on, we'll discover that Brad and Tim have gotten an EVP on two different voice recorders. It seems to say the words: *"Susan is dead."*

However, *Susan* comes through over and over again. There's no context, but the name appears to be of some kind of significance. Tim asks for clarification and the response comes back as both *"Sister"* and an emphatic *"Shut up!"*

Then things turn profane. *"Fuck!"* he declares with vehemence.

"This is the first time I've heard you swear," Tim shakes his head, fighting to suppress a smile.

"We're supposed to," Brad responds, before adding, *"Fighting."*

"Who are you fighting?"

There's no reply. A long pause. Then: *"Susan has it!"*

"Has what?"

"That's it. End."

Tim sounds disappointed. "Are you ending the conversation?"

"No."

If anything, Brad's tone of voice has gotten more forceful and emphatic...but the meaning is no clearer.

"Zoot Suit," Tim says, which has us both scratching our heads. That's a very weirdly specific thing to say. Zoot Suits were a style of male clothing that became ubiquitous back in the 1920s through 1940s and can be seen in films from that period. The high-waisted, baggy suits were most popular with African Americans and Canadian males. They were worn by men who wanted to appear stylish, particularly musicians, performers and dancers...the type of guys who would go to jazz clubs and dances at places like this house once was.

"Hello!" Brad booms, followed once again by: *"That's it."*

I join the session at this point, just in time for Brad to welcome me with a very loud: *"Fat pig!"*

Rude, admittedly, but weighing in at three hundred pounds, I'm not going to argue with him.

"Shit. Pussy." The profanity continues. Tim and I exchange a look. Whatever the source of communication is, it's unlikely to be commercial radio. *"Fuck this!"*

"Eff what — are you talking about this conversation?" Tim wants to know.

"Is that it?" Brad fires back almost immediately. *"Forest."*

We get the word "forest" three times over the space of just a few minutes. The AI app pings, heralding the arrival of a new image, this one depicting a lush green forest beside a calm blue lake.

"Susan! Susan says...!" Brad's tone has become a little more urgent.

"I'm getting chills," mutters Tim.

Then there's a *second* image of trees around the periphery of a body of water. Two in rapid succession, over the space of just three minutes.

"Suspect. Susan."

Whoever Susan might be, somebody *really* wants us to be aware of her. Is she a suspect in some kind of crime, perhaps one which took place near a forested lake? Or are we simply reading too much into what may in reality be just a series of random and unrelated data points?

We just don't know.

The words Brad's putting out trail off into apparent randomness. It seems as though somebody was trying to tell their story but wasn't quite able to get it across. I hit upon the idea of having the other group come up here and see what they get, on the premise that a fresh set of personalities and infusion of new and different energies probably won't hurt.

"Susan came through *a lot*," Brad observes, blinking rapidly as his eyes readjust to the light. This has been one of the longest Estes

Sessions I've ever been part of, clocking in at almost forty minutes — close to double the usual duration.

Our team congregates downstairs. We're met at the foot of the staircase by Satan, who's wagging his tail laconically. Everybody gives his ears a scratch as we pass by.

There are snacks and some idle chit chat, but each group makes a point of not sharing any details about what happened on each of their respective floors.

Brad has the sudden urge to do a quick solo EVP session on the third floor while the rest of us are snacking. He disappears, only to return five minutes later with a frown on his face. The batteries in his digital voice recorder, which were brand new out of the packaging and loaded into the device only an hour ago, are totally and utterly dead. Assuming that this isn't a defective batch of batteries, which is very rare, such unexplained power drains are often precursors of paranormal activity and make me optimistic for what the coming day might have in store.

After fifteen minutes have passed, so we switcheroo. Stephen, Jill, and Rob go on up to the third floor, while Brad, Tim and I relocate to the Speakeasy.

This time out, Brad will be the questioner while Tim goes under the hood for an Estes session. We gather around the table, and I set both my tablet and voice recorder atop it.

"This looks like a nice place to have a drink," Brad observes. "Did you imbibe?"

"It's me," Tim responds.

"Who's me? My name's Brad. This is Richard. We're here to speak with you."

"Wait."

"For what?" Brad clears his throat, leaning back in his chair.

"Warning!" That's followed by *"Blumberg."*

Brad and I trade looks. Is there some kind of warning in store for the family?

"Can you hear us?" Brad asks, after Tim reels off a series of apparently meaningless words.

"No. No!" Tim says, emphasizing the second word. Then: *"Liar! Bye."*

Brad frowns and asks who's leaving.

What comes next is profane to the extreme: it's what I'll only refer to as "the C-word." Brad asks who's being referred to. Tim replies with: *"Poor baby,"* then *"several bodies."*

"What was done to the bodies down here?"

"Look out! Look out!"

Now that *definitely* seems like a warning. The question is — a warning about what?

There's movement from the corner of my eye. A big, bearded apparition appears in the doorway. It's Arryn, giving someone a quick tour of the house.

"Sorry for interrupting," he says politely.

"The human sacrifice got here just in time," deadpans Brad. Arryn and his guest beat a hasty retreat.

"Listen!" Tim insists. *"Can you hear it?"*

Whoever's speaking with him seems annoyed that we were temporarily distracted.

"Again — Michael!"

I jot down the name, alongside that of Susan, in case it should prove to be relevant later on.

"Death," Tim adds. Brad inquires whether it's possible for us to speak with the dead and is told: *"It doesn't help."*

Ping. The screen of my tablet depicts an image of bright red blood splattered across a clinical-looking tile floor. Very apropos for an embalming room.

"Daddy, I'm hungry," says Tim. Although it doesn't raise eyebrows at the time, it's only with the benefit of hindsight and the contextualization of the *"...Daddy"* EVP we recorded right here the day before, that I start to think we might be dealing with the spirit of a child...more specifically, that of a little girl.

At least, something that *sounds* like one...

"Liar," Tim shudders, then switches out of his Estes voice. "Screaming. I just heard screaming. *Shut up!"*

"Yeah, Richard, shut the hell up!" Brad snorts, laughing.

"You shut your..." Tim agrees.

Somebody, it seems, is growing increasingly irritated with us.

"What do you like to drink?" Brad asks, changing gears.

"Ninety."

"Ninety proof?" Brad asks.

"Yup."

Alcoholic beverages that are 90% percent proof *do* exist. However, nobody drinks them because they actually *like* them. That would be like developing a taste for brake fluid or antifreeze. They exist for one purpose, and one purpose only: to get the imbiber as hammered as possible, as quickly as possible, and imbibing them in any meaningful sort of quantity runs the risk of killing the drinker, or at the very least rendering them comatose. They contain 45% alcohol. We're now either talking to a hardcore drinker or somebody is pulling our collective leg.

Still, I suspect that if I poured Brad and Tim a shot of it, they'd both down it like the proverbial rockstars, burning pain in the esophagus be damned.

(Writer's note: if you must drink, and it goes without saying that you should only ever drink responsibly, then may I respectfully suggest avoiding the 90% proof jet fuel, and taking some time to sample the delightful drink recipes provided by Arryn which are distributed throughout this book?)

"Maybe tonight," Tim begins, in a tone of voice that has suddenly turned quite sinister, *"we'll come out..."*

Promises, promises. We'd like nothing better than a little company for the evening.

"Hold me," continues Tim, followed by the dubious: *"Party on! Pussy! Pussy!"*

Well, things have definitely gone to an entirely less pleasant level now. There are F-bombs and other profanities. If this is a spirit communicator, then we're dealing with somebody with a bad temperament and a fast lifestyle (at least, when they last *had* a life).

"Look at me!"

Brad makes a show of looking around the Speakeasy. "Where are you?"

"Angel. Demon. Demon. Are you listening?"

"Yes," Brad responds, "but we don't see any angels or demons."

"We believe. Sadness! Wrong! DADDY!"

There's that word again. Somebody calling for their daddy.

"It's time. Thank you very much."

"It's time for what?" Brad asks.

"The truth. Hold on..."

"We're waiting for the truth." Brad clears his throat.

"Zoot Suit," Tim says. Now that *is* interesting. The same extremely specific, very niche phrase, which Brad heard upstairs on the third floor, and is now being repeated by a different listener three floors

below. *Zoot Suit* isn't a term you hear very often, so to hear it spoken twice in the same place on the same day seems noteworthy.

So is what comes next: "Egypt."

I sit bolt upright in my chair, remembering that Jill's recent visit to Egypt was brought up at this very table just the night before...when neither Brad nor Tim was present. Neither did any of us tell them about that particular interaction.

"Who went to Egypt?" Brad wants to know.

"Somebody else," Tim replies. He's absolutely right about that.

Brad asks what color the Zoot Suit was. Tim replies by demanding that everybody say the Lord's Prayer and exhorts us to *"believe."* Checking his watch, Brad realizes that almost forty minutes have passed again. It's time to bring Tim out, which Brad does by tapping his buddy on the arm.

Tim listening to a spirit box in the Speakeasy.

Startled at the unexpected touch, Tim removes the headphones and sets them down. We can still hear the loud, staticky noise coming through until I reach out and switch the box off.

"That felt like I was listening to several different conversations at once," he tells us. "Difficult to make a lot of it out. There was a really heavy feeling at one point, when I heard the words *angel* and *demon*. It felt so oppressive that I actually said some prayers myself, internally."

Tim's a solid investigator and is not one that's given to flights of fancy. If whatever it was that he experienced was so disturbing to him that he felt compelled to pray, I'm certainly going to treat it with respect and a due amount of caution.

While we were being sworn down in the basement, Rob, Jill and Stephen were investigating up on the third floor. They're determined to track down the mysterious book which Jill's pendulum told them had a spirit attachment latched onto it. She uses the same technique browsing among Noa's collection of books.

Rob is running the same AI app that I've been trialing. He's in Noa's bedroom. The first image that comes through is the silhouette of a young girl sitting on a bed in front of a window. The resemblance to his present environment is striking.

After much yes and no pendulum-based book hunting, Jill finally hits upon the object of her quest. It's a book called *The Witch's Book of Self-Care*, part of Noa's personal library. She asks whether the spirit attachment is able to manipulate things physically in this room, and does it do so whenever Noa's here? The answer supplied by the pendulum is yes.

"Have you always been attached to that book?" Stephen wants to know. Yes again.

Jill asks whether this is the spirit that's responsible for expecting the lights, and is told that in fact, that's another entity...a male spirit. *This* communicator is also a male, but he is not the man that Heather has seen walking throughout the house. They make a note to tell Noa about the book and what the pendulum says about it, then let her make her own mind up as to how best it ought to be dealt with. This is, after all, Noa's turf and it's her decision as to what happens in here.

However, there's some confusion going on because this book wasn't inventory in Heather's store. It's part of Noa's personal collection. Do the spirits have their wires crossed — or do we?

When we gather together again in the kitchen, I let Jill know about Egypt having come up during the Estes session. Heather's ears perk up. "I have an artifact in the house that comes from Egypt. It's part of an antique camel saddle which she acquired just over a month ago...and it's sitting at the top of the staircase that leads down to the Speakeasy.

Well, you know what they say about assumptions...

Perhaps that artifact has an attachment all of its own. Perhaps the "Egypt" comments are directed toward Jill. Or possibly a little of Column A and a little of Column B. Clearly, more digging is required, and yet, we have so much ground still to cover inside this house, we've barely even begun to scratch the surface.

Chapter Fourteen

Arryn's Adult Beverages - This is Halloween!

*T**his is Halloween!*

   1. *1.5 oz Mount Gay Eclipse Rum (or another great Caribbean rum, but Barbados will always have our heart)*

2.   *0.5 oz Grand Marnier*

3.   *0.25 oz Aperol*

   (This gives the drink a fantastic bitter note and a stunning orange color, just right for the spooky time of year)

4.   *1 oz fresh squeezed orange juice*

   Add a tiny pinch of Maldon salt to the orange juice so it dissolves properly before you shake it

5.   *0.25 oz fresh squeezed lemon juice*

6.   *2-3 drops Angostura Orange Bitters*

7.   *1-2 drops Arz Orange Blossom water*

8.   An egg white from a small-medium egg

   Use really good eggs! Ideally something from a farmers' market that you know are fresh

9.   Add all the booze, juice and egg white to a big shaker, NO ice at this stage

   Egg whites create volume so be sure to use a big shaker and have a bar towel on hand

10.   Now you can shake this like crazy trying to create a froth creamy drink or you can use a cappuccino frother - those little circular electric whiskeys that you can put into a coffee cup

11.   Get this mixture good and mixed then add ice, give it another good shake to get the cocktail super cold

12.   Strain into a chilled coupe glass

   If you have done this right, you should have a nice creamy head on the cocktail much like you would with a well poured Guinness

13.   Express an orange peel over the top of the cocktail (i.e. squeeze the peel lengthwise so all the oils are squeezed out over the top)

   This is a very important step! If you don't do this the drink will smell of egg as you lift it to drink...not pleasant!

   If you want to be **really** fancy, you can flame the peel as you express with a match so the oils burn just a bit - don't use a lighter as the gas will destroy the oils' flavor

14.   Garnish by floating a dehydrated orange round on the top of the cocktail

15.   Drink with satisfaction having made something pretty complicated

Chapter Fifteen

Heather Goes Under

B earing in mind that the two most active parts of the house seem to be the third floor and the basement, next on our agenda is further investigation of Noa's living space. This time, we're going to work as one big group.

As we settle in for the next half hour, we can hear the wind howling around the eaves.

First under the Estes hood is our man, Rob. He slips easily into the near-trance state that the technique often induces.

Stephen opens what we hope will be a conversation by saying hello and asking whether there's anybody around who's willing to communicate.

"Hey," Rob says, repeating what he's hearing through the spirit box.

Game on.

After a minute of silence, Stephen asks: "Is there anybody here who'd like to talk?"

"Yes." Rob's speaking in a slow, drawn-out tone of voice, one which seems feminine to my ear. This is confirmed seconds later when he adds: *"Hi.* Woman's voice."

"Hello. Can you tell me how many are up here?"

Rob frowns, screwing his face up in concentration. "That was a woman's voice. Couldn't hear exactly what she was saying."

"Did you have your funeral here at this house?"

"Leave," comes the firm answer. "Woman's voice again."

"Are you saying you want to us to leave?"

In response, Rob hears a woman laughing, followed by the words *"Get out."*

Bing. I glance down at my tablet screen. It shows the face of an old woman, crone-like in the style of the stereotypical hag from fable.

Then he hears a little girl asking for help. *"Cold"* and *"dead"* are followed by *"need help."*

"Where are you? We need to find you so we can help you," Stephen replies.

"In here. Look up."

"The Widow's Walk?"

"Look up," Rob repeats. We do. All that's above us is indeed the roof.

His next remark is *"planchette,"* which begs the question of whether we'd have better luck communicating by using a talking board, instead of the Estes Method. I ask, and I'm rebuffed with *"Get out!"* Rob adds that this was a different voice to the woman who initially said it to us.

Either somebody doesn't like Ouija boards, somebody doesn't like us...or both.

"Pool," Rob deadpans.

"Did you drown?" replies Stephen.

"I died. Dead."

"Did you die in the pool?"

"Poooooooollll…" It's a long, drawn-out response, delivered in an eerie tone of voice somewhat akin to that of a person who is either medicated, intoxicated, or deeply confused. Right on its heels, Stephen's question seems to be answered with a curt: *"Yep."*

"How old were you?" Stephen asks gently.

The answer hits us like a sucker punch to the gut.

"Three."

There is much shaking of heads. We are all either parents, aunts, or uncles. Thinking about a three-year-old child drowning is beyond awful.

"Was it this pool, the one here at the house?"

We're dreading that the answer will be yes. *"Cold,"* comes the response.

"Do you have anybody with you?"

"Rob."

That's a true statement. Whoever they are, they do indeed have Rob with them.

"Whoever you are, it would really help us to know your name," coaxes Stephen. Rob's answer is gruff and borderline hostile.

"Male voice. *Get out!*"

Again with the get out.

"No," Stephen demurs politely but firmly. "We're not. What is your name?"

"Richard." This is spoken by the same male voice, Rob will later reveal.

"Richard, what is the little girl's name?"

"I'm hearing a little girl humming," Rob reports. "Maybe…*Heidi*?"

"Can you give me the exact number of how many spirits are here?"

The answer is immediate. *"Three."*

"How do you feel right now?"

"Cool."

"Temperature-wise?" Stephen is seeking clarification.

"Yep."

"...and is there any light where you are?"

"It's dark."

This back and forth is very impressive. There's no way Rob can possibly hear our questions over the incessant chatter of the spirit box. He can't see through the blind fold, and even if he could, Stephen is sitting behind him, so lip reading would be out of the question. The appropriate and timely responses strongly suggest that there's a form of paranormal communication going on right now, and the team is stoked to be a part of it.

"Hi, everyone! New voice. Woman's voice." Rob has a new speaker up on deck. She sounds much cheerier than the previous communicators.

"How's your day so far?" Stephen asks.

"Good."

"Everything going okay?"

"Yes."

"How strong do you feel? The reason I'm asking is...I'd very much like it if you could either tap on the wall or get this chandelier to swing a little bit." Stephen points up at the light fixture dangling from the ceiling.

"Stop," Rob says.

Lo and behold, the spirit box dies, right here and now. It's gotten just two hours' worth of usage on a fresh battery, which would normally keep it going for at least two or three times that long.

Rob takes off the headphones and blindfold, and we clue him in on our side of the conversation. He admits to feeling a little bit drained after the session, we ran for twenty-five minutes. We're all impressed by how on-point the questions and answers seemed to be. Nobody doubts that we were just engaged in a very real conversation with somebody that none of us can see.

Tim and Brad want to try conducting an Estes session by themselves in Noa's space. Brad will be the listener this time out, while Tim asks the questions.

They start out by introducing themselves to the spirits again. There's no reason to assume that they'll necessarily be communicating with the same speakers as yesterday, or earlier today.

A quick burst EVP session precedes their main experiment. It yields nothing but the sound of their own voices asking questions. After seven minutes, it's time for them to begin using the Estes Method.

"The tablet," is Brad's opening statement.

"If you mean the one that can draw pictures, we don't have it with us right now," Tim explains. He's jotting down notes on a tablet of his own, but it doesn't have the AI app loaded on it.

"Institute. Inside."

"Were you put in an institution?"

"Prison," Brad confirms, which tells Tim that they probably aren't speaking with a child this time. *"Help me. Six..."*

"Six? Is that the number of people here right now, or is it your age—"

"SICK!" Brad corrects him, impatience and frustration both evident in his voice. *"Vomit."*

After a period of what seem like random, incoherent words, Brad comes out with: *"Must get up. Heart attack..."*

Tim seeks clarification, but the unseen speaker won't be drawn further on this subject. That's understandable. Not every spirit communicator wants to talk about the manner and specifics of their death, necessarily. Doing so could involve reliving an intensely traumatic memory, potentially the most traumatic thing that has ever happened to them. Understanding this, Tim backs away from this line of questioning and returns to safer, more generic ground — but he's interrupted.

"Get out!"

"We're not leaving—" Tim begins.

"Leave. Now!" Brad is insistent. Not wanting to push the issue any further, Tim decides that discretion is the better part of valor. He starts the process of bringing the session to a close.

"Messed up. Suicide."

Just as he's about to quit, Brad hears the sound of another speaker dropping in, announcing themselves with the name *Peyton*.

"Hi, Peyton," says Tim, crossing one knee over the other and continuing to enter notes onto his tablet. "I'm Tim. This is Brad. We'd love to talk to you."

"Fuck you."

"Peyton — why would you say that?" Tim remains calm, but he also adopts the same tone of voice a parent would use when addressing an unruly child.

Peyton, it seems, is not very nice.

"It's all a test," Brad says.

"Oh, really?"

Tim barely has time to get his question out before Brad cuts him off with: *"Yeah."* After that comes: *"Thief! Thief!"*

What follows makes little to no sense. Finally, looking at his watch and seeing that Brad has been under for thirty minutes, he tells Peyton and his cohort that it's time for them to quit.

"See ya," Brad dismisses him.

"We *will* see you," Tim says affably, tapping his partner on the knee. Brad comes back to the everyday world, and the two men spend a few minutes discussing the session. Their conclusion is...inconclusive. Although there is a new name to research, and some apparently intelligent responses, nothing new has been learned. That's just the way it goes sometimes. Jill, Stephen, Rob and I have spent this period of time investigating some more of the objects in Heather's shop. Other than seeing some things we'd each quite like to buy, we haven't learned anything new either.

Unwilling to focus on the same areas over and over, our next stop is the master bedroom and adjoining bathroom on the second floor. Although there aren't many accounts of paranormal activity associated with this part of the house, we're working on the premise that you never know until you try.

Jill deploys some cat balls on the floor in the bathroom and on the bedroom floor. These little gadgets are easy to obtain and are very affordable. They're little transparent spheres which, once they're set off by the energy of vibration, will flash a sequence of bright colors. Paranormal enthusiasts use them as potential trigger items during an investigation, inviting spirits to set them off via direct physical interaction.

Each of us finds a spot on the cool tile floor. We sit in silence for a few minutes, just acclimating to the environment and letting it get used to us in return.

Eight minutes into our watch, the cat ball farthest from us in the master bedroom begins flashing. Nobody is in there, or indeed, up here on the second floor at all. It takes a certain degree of force to set a cat ball off. Somebody walking around downstairs, or even elsewhere on this floor, is highly unlikely to do it. You'd have to walk past the cat ball at a fairly short distance in order to do it.

Rob and Jill invite whoever might have triggered it to come and spend some time with us. Unfortunately, nobody accepts our offer...or so it appears at first. We sit around for a while, just shooting the breeze and running our voice recorders. This kind of informal banter is, we've found, one of the best ways to get interaction from our unseen companions — far more so than the stuffy and formal approach, we many of us are taught (or adopt from Hollywood movies and TV shows) when we first start out in the field.

With nothing much going on, after a while we elect to relocate back to the room in which the hanging took place. Unbeknownst to us, however, it appears that we *did* have some company in the master bathroom. It's only when I play back the audio recording during the evidence review phase that I hear a female voice, speaking directly after Stephen and Jill, forcefully hissing the word *"STOP!"*

The voice clearly doesn't belong to Jill. Not only does it sound different to her speaking voice, but Jill would have had absolutely no reason to say that word during our investigative session. For the purposes of due diligence, once the potential EVP is discovered, Jill tries her hardest to replicate it. She is unable to. Her very best effort sounds nothing like it.

Apparently, somebody didn't like what we were doing in that bathroom. After the EVP, they completely clammed up. No other anomalies would turn up on the recording after that one. But it's enough. It was crystal clear and so loud that whoever spoke that word sounded as if they were very close to the digital voice recorder, which

I had set up in the middle of the bathroom floor, roughly equidistant from each investigator.

Although I'm not at liberty to share details, I can say that the master bathroom was at one time subdivided into two bedrooms. According to conversations Heather has had with people who are connected to the house and its history, at one time, a female resident died in one of those two bedrooms. Although this is admittedly hearsay, when viewed in the light of the woman's voice turning up as an EVP, it becomes harder to dismiss it as a coincidence.

Stephen, Jill, Rob and I all remain blissfully unaware of this as we once again take up positions inside the room in which a former occupant is said to have hanged themselves. We settle in and begin to ask questions, once again attempting to make contact with whoever may be around.

Forty-five minutes later, all we have to show for our time are various instances of gastrointestinal discomfort recorded for posterity on our voice recorders. There are no EVPs, no odd phenomena, nothing noteworthy whatsoever.

At the conclusion of the session, we're treated to a sumptuous home-cooked meal courtesy of our hosts. In pride of place on the menu is a chili and rice dish which I suspect is going to contaminate our audio recordings even more than they already have been. Giving the entire team platefuls of spicy food is a bold choice, to say the least, and we'll probably come to regret it later on.

After dinner, I take a stroll out to the pool. Standing on the edge, I can't help wondering about the drowning comments and references to "pool" that took place during Brad and Tim's Estes session earlier. It's not solid enough to make a definitive connection, but it's also possible that more evidence might arise later to shed more light on things.

When I bring this up to Heather, she reminds me that one local resident had said that a woman did indeed drown in this swimming pool. That sends a chill down my spine. I'd heard this before, and completely forgotten it, the nugget of information having somehow gotten misfiled in the dank, cluttered morass of my middle-aged mind.

Suddenly, I'm looking at the empty swimming pool in an entirely different way.

Our next order of business is a return to the Speakeasy. We're going downstairs *en masse* this time.

For the first time, we're involving the Blumbergs directly in the investigation of their own home. Ever since the first signs of ghostly goings-on, Heather and Noa have been fascinated at the probability that the funeral home is haunted. Now, having watched our activities on day one, they're eager to get hands-on themselves. We're only too happy to oblige.

Brad's recorder has once again died, having burned through another set of brand-new batteries in no time at all. Heather reveals that during the filming of *We Bought a Funeral Home,* there were so many unexplained battery drains that the production crew had to bring in extra batteries and chargers in order to keep up with them. In fact, additional power outlets had to be installed to service them. We've had multiple battery-powered devices die during our two days here, and the only thing we can say for sure is that the energy has to be going *somewhere.* Could it be being used to fuel the paranormal activity that's taking place inside the house? It's a reasonable hypothesis, and one that many members of the paranormal community would find easy to accept.

We coach Heather on how to be the listener during an Estes Method session, explaining what she'll be hearing and how she should repeat it verbally, as best she can. She nods her understanding and takes a seat, bathed in the red glow which pervades the Speakeasy. First the blindfold and then the headphones are put into place, and the spirit box is configured with the same settings we've been using throughout our investigation.

Then we're off.

"I'm hearing a woman's voice," she tells us hesitantly.

From somewhere down below, there's a growl. For the first time in my career as a paranormal investigator, I get to use the phrase "tagging Satan" for my audio recording. There's a corresponding thump of a heavy tail hitting the floor in response.

"Out!" Heather says, her tone of voice containing an edge of steel that wasn't there seconds ago. *"She's here! Leaving."*

Heather points to her right side, indicating we know not what.

"Going where?" Brad wants to know.

"I have hands on my shoulders," Heather shivers. I look and confirm that there's nobody visible behind her, just empty space.

"This is your first ever opportunity to communicate with Heather like this," I address the invisible toucher. "What do you want to say to her?"

She's hearing an indistinct male voice, but she can't make out anything that he's saying...until: *"Stop!"*

It is repeated two more times, with increasing urgency.

Just like the EVP we recorded in the master bathroom, somebody seems to be unhappy with what we're doing. Nevertheless, we press on.

"Somebody...a woman...is shushing me," Heather explains, sounding a little frustrated. *"Shush!"*

"What is it that you don't want us to know?" I ask in a low voice.

There's a low growl. It's Beans, apparently taking exception to the presence of something which none of us can see. Perhaps we have a visitor.

"Are you shushing us, or somebody else here that we can't see?" Brad seeks clarification.

"*STOP!*"

We don't. Never before have the spirits of the house had an opportunity to connect with one of the Blumbergs directly in this way. I'm determined to give them the chance to make themselves heard, but it's looking increasingly as though at least one of them wants to shut the others up.

Somebody doesn't want us to know something. The question is — who, and what?

"Why are you here?" Stephen asks.

"*You! You!*" Heather sounds increasingly unhappy, becoming a little breathless despite the fact that she's just sitting there, repeating what she's hearing. "*Ssh! Ssshhh!*"

"We're getting close to time," Stephen observes, looking at his watch.

"A man just said *Goodbye*," Heather announces.

We bring her out, tapping her lightly to end the session.

"It felt as if there was a bright light in my face throughout the entire thing," Heather says, coming back to the comfortable red ambience of the Speakeasy. Of course, no lights were on her at any time. What she experienced was perhaps a side effect of sensory deprivation. Her hands are trembling slightly.

"How was it?"

"Really unsettling. A young woman came through. Pale skin. Dark haired, pulled back away from her face. Standing right next to me. I could see her in my mind's eye. About 25 years old. Slim build.

Then I felt hands on my shoulders, even through the back of the chair, pushing down on me. I was also aware of a man standing right there." She points at where I'm sitting. "Totally different feeling between the two of them. He went after a little while. She stayed through the entire thing."

I'm beginning to think that Heather may have some degree of psychic sensitivity.

"Neither of them was entirely welcoming," she goes on. "I think she was the one shushing and telling us to stop."

"So, were they talking to one another, or talking to us?" I ask.

"It felt directed at us," Heather says, after considering it for a moment. "At me specifically. She felt frustrated, annoyed...I think I was the one who they wanted to shut up."

Heather heard her own name clearly, and a second female name in addition to that — Ellen. The name goes into our data log.

Now that she has her first ever Estes Method session in the bag, Heather has earned herself a break. Policing up our equipment, we go back up to the kitchen for refreshments.

Once again, this house has given us more questions than answers. It's starting to seem as though we're opening an enormous can of worms.

Lunch gives us the opportunity to try something I've never eaten before but heard a lot about: poutine. For those who've never tried it, imagine a plate full of French Fries (chips, if you're British) slathered in cheese curds and gravy. Poutine looks like an absolute mess, and it is. It's also carbohydrate heaven, and you can feel your coronary arteries narrowing with each and every forkful.

Properly fortified, we buckle down for an afternoon and evening of further investigation. Stephen, Rob, Jill and I are focusing on the Speakeasy again. Stephen believes it's the most energetically active part of the house at the moment, and short of a better lead, I'm willing to give his hunch a shot.

Jill sets up an EM pump, a gadget with the sole purpose of flooding the environment with electromagnetic energy. Some have hypothesized that this additional power may act as a kind of "ghost buffet," allowing spirits to manifest more easily or powerfully.

Rob deploys a Parascope, which is designed to measure static electricity levels. Upon detecting a rise in this environmental direct current (DC) energy, the device lights up one of eight probes in a color that correlates to the strength of that energy. Long story short: increased static DC energy equals flashing lights, which may or may not be paranormal in nature. For example, the huge thunderstorm we recently experienced could definitely have set the Parascope off, as increased static electricity levels are part of the way such storms manifest. That's why this particular gadget is only coming out now, with the weather relatively clear and environmental conditions stable.

"Oh, my goodness!" Jill sounds startled. She's pointing at Rob. Blinking rapidly, she explains that for just a split second, she caught sight of a figure sitting right next to him. It was there one instant and gone the next. In the low-level red light of the Speakeasy, it's possible that this was just a trick of the light...then again, perhaps one of the spirits of the funeral home has decided to join us for a while. I hope it's the latter.

Stephen fires up an app which fills the Speakeasy with choppy fragments of noise that are very heavy on the reverb. The app, which I won't name, is controversial. He's a believer in its ability to convey messages from the other side. It's fair to say that I lean more skeptical towards it. Although I've heard it say some incredible things on occasion, I believe that much of what comes out of it is probably audio pareidolia — the listener's brain desperately attempting to make sense out of what is really nothing more than a meaningless jumble of sound, the auditory equivalent of a Jackson Pollock painting.

There's room for multiple different schools of thought on this investigation, and I'm happy to let Stephen's app show us what it can do. We run the AI app alongside it, to see if the two pieces of software will synchronize their results in some way.

They don't.

Jill asks for somebody to tell us something meaningful. All we get in response is a series of harsh, guttural soundbites. Stephen thinks he's hearing words, but if that's true, it's not reaching my ears in the same way. Different strokes for different folks, as the saying goes. At the end of half an hour, I don't think we have much to show for it.

Maybe, I muse, it's time for a different approach.

While Jill, Stephen Rob and I are off doing our own thing, Tim and Brad down to the Speakeasy once more. It's a part of the building that we all feel drawn to. I'm in agreement with Becky that the most paranormally active parts of the house so far are Noa's third floor lair and the old embalming space. It follows a certain sort of logic, to my mind at least, that this basement level would most likely be the epicenter of the haunting. For one thing, there are seemingly countless hypotheses which associate paranormal activity with rock, soil, and the water table. You're closer to all of those things down here in the Speakeasy than we would be anywhere else in the house.

Tim and Brad each take a seat in one of the gleaming barber chairs, making themselves comfortable. They each set out a recorder at various points around the room, intending to cover as much of the sound-space as possible with microphones.

The first order of business is a burst EVP session, which Brad initiates. He talks about the panoply of medical apparatus which can be found all around the newly furnished cigar lounge.

Tim and Brad alternate their questions, asking what the spirits make of the transformation of the former embalming room into a place of recreation. It's a fair point. Yet if the spectral residents have any opinion, they seem unwilling to share it. We don't pick up EVPs on any of our recorders. Perhaps there's nobody here right now. Maybe the happening place to be is upstairs, instead of down here in the basement with some middle-aged dudes.

The next session takes place next to the casket bar, which sits atop the elevator once used to lift the real thing up and down between floors. The lads get some Rem-Pod hits almost immediately after relocating to the Speakeasy. However, it's a long, continuous stream of light and noise, which suggests that the cause is most likely a depleted battery. The half-life of most batteries in this house is abnormally low.

The questions this time around are a little more general, asking about the weather, what occupation the potential communicator might have had during their lifetime, whether they had any children, and so forth. Essentially, small talk.

Brad gestures expansively toward the illuminated casket and the rows of liquor bottles it contains.

"This is quite an extensive selection. If you imbibed, what was your drink of choice?"

"I personally *love* a good gin and tonic," Tim adds encouragingly.

"I prefer beer," Brad admits.

When they play the recording back, we're disappointed to find that none of the resident spirits has joined in to offer their own personal preference.

"Feels quiet," says Brad. He's right. It is.

After half an hour passes with absolutely nothing to show for it, Brad and Tim gather up their equipment and head for the stairs.

There are footsteps on the ground floor and the now common chorus of barking dogs announces the arrival of a visitor: it's Becky, who cleans the house, and has a number of strange experiences of her own to share with us. We meet her in the Chapel. Introductions are made, and then we all sit down for an interview.

Becky Adams ("like Sam Adams, not the Addams Family") knows virtually every nook and cranny of the property; after all, she has dusted, swept, and vacuumed much of it. One day, she answered an ad looking for somebody to clean a former funeral home in Dresden. That somebody was of course Heather, Keeping the colossal residence clean is no small task. Becky has her work cut out for her.

"Doesn't it bother you, knowing what this place used to be in the past?" I ask. Becky shakes her head.

"No. People were dead before they ever came here. There's nothing to be scared of."

"Other than whatever clogged up the drains." I'm half joking, but part of me suspects that the plumbing system of a business which performs embalming as part of its services might get a little...shall we say, overly stressed at times.

"This place is very peaceful to me," Becky goes on. "Very calming. I'm here all by myself some days, sometimes for eight hours at a stretch."

The first inkling she had that something strange was going on came in the form of a woman's voice calling out "Hello!" It usually happened when she was cleaning an upper floor of the house. The voice always came from somewhere beneath her, possibly the ground floor. It was a friendly greeting. There was nothing threatening about it. At first, just as Arryn had, Becky thought that it might have been Heather calling out to her. She soon learned that this was not the case.

Two weeks ago, the same thing happened again — but this time, the voice calling out inside the empty house belonged to a man, not a woman.

I find Becky to be a credible witness. She doesn't exaggerate, nor make things out to be more than they are. She has no stories of seeing apparitions, being touched by invisible hands, or anything particularly creepy. The voices are all she has experienced so far, and when it comes to credibility, sometimes less is more.

The only thing that she is afraid of within these walls are bats.

"I think there are spirits here," Becky tells us, before correcting herself. "In fact, I *know* they're here."

"How? How do you know?"

"Because they said *Hello*, Richard!" Brad cuts in, with mock exasperation.

"You can just sense them," Becky smiles. "You can feel their presence sometimes."

This leads me to ask her which parts of the house is that presence felt most strongly. After considering for a moment, she singles out Noa's room and the Speakeasy. Nobody has told her about her experiences in the house thus far; the fact that these have been our two most active areas is unknown to her. This comes as a form of validation.

"They're just over your shoulder in those areas," she tells us. Presumably just standing there. Watching.

I appreciate the fact that Becky acknowledges the presence of spirits within the house, and that she doesn't find it to be scary or intimidating. She shares her experiences and offers her opinions thoughtfully, in a matter-of-fact way.

Thanking Becky for her time, I turn off the voice recorder I reserve for interviews and set it carefully into my equipment bag.

"You've got to be open to this kind of thing, or they won't show up," Becky advises me. "They just won't show up."

Fortunately for us, they've been showing up aplenty so far. Fingers crossed that they continue to do so as our investigation rolls into its next phase.

Chapter Sixteen

Arryn's Adult Beverages - Something Spicy This Way Comes

Something *Spicy This Way Comes*

1. 2 oz Cazadores Tequila Anejo (or another great *anejo* tequila)

2. 0.25 oz Casamigos Mezcal (or another mezcal to give that hint of smoke)

3. 0.25 oz Grand Marnier (you can use Cointreau but as the other ingredients are fancy...)

4. 2-3 drops Fee Brothers Habanero Bitters (if you don't have this don't worry, a few drops Orange or even normal bitters of you choice works just as well)

5.   1 oz Fresh pineapple juice (you can juice your own, but I just buy a carton as long as it has no added sugar and isn't a lite version)

6.   0.25 oz Fresh squeezed lime juice with a small pinch of Maldon salt dissolved in

7   .0.25 oz Spicy pineapple syrup

8.   Spicy Pineapple Syrup

9.   Add 1 cup of water to ¾ cup dark brown sugar and ¼ cup honey to a pot

10.   Start to warm the pot over a medium heat, you don't want to boil it just dissolve everything

11.   Add about 2 cups of fresh pineapple to the water as it warms, I like to use a just over-ripe pineapple, so the flavour is really intense

12.   Add ¼ cup of jalapenos cut into rounds to the water, I do deseed mostly because if you don't, they clog the cocktail shakers spout when you pour (Taste the jalapenos when you first cut them as some have lots of heat and others are totally bland)

13.   Add ¼ cup of habaneros or scotch bonnet cut into rounds to the water

14.   Slowly let this all warm up while the sugar and honey dissolves

15.   I taste at this point, if not spicy enough for you add some chili flakes if it's not sweet enough add a touch more sugar

16.   Once everything has come to a simmer, turn off the heat and let it sit for at least an hour until its cooled and had a chance for the flavors to develop

17.   Strain into a container, ideally one with a lid

18.   Keep the pineapple and chili rounds to be used as garnish

19.   Add all the ingredients into a big shaker full of ice and get the work out you avoided earlier in the day by shaking a lot!

20.   Pineapple, like egg whites, will create volume as you shake them and create a creamy head on the drink when poured

21. Taste the cocktail before you serve as each pineapple and chili will bring more or less of its flavor, add more syrup if it is needs or more lime etc. to balance the drink

22. Shake again

23. Pour into a chilled small margarita glass or a coup glass - NO ice

24. Garnish with a piece of the pineapple used to make the syrup

25. Drink in trepidation of how spicy this might be and how it will build

Chapter Seventeen

Shush!

A good night's sleep sets everybody up for success. On the morning of day three, we once again gather for a breakfast bagel and some wake-up juice to start the day out right. Once again, we do the vehicular shuffle from hotel to motel to AirBnB, assembling our motley crew for what we hope will be another exciting day at the Blumberg residence.

It's a school day, so Noa is out of the house, but Raff, Arryn and Heather are there to greet us, along with the all-important pup squad. There's no welcome quite like those which come with slobbery tongues and wagging tails.

Heather is still abuzz from her first experience with the Estes Method, and she's eager to try it again. Raff, one of the in-house skeptics, is also willing to give it a shot, which I'm rather looking forward to. I'm dying to find out whether his default state of open-minded skepticism will make the communicators more or less likely to interact with him.

As a collective, we all want to focus on Noa's room first. The Speakeasy was relatively quiet yesterday, by comparison, and nobody has been down there since. That means there has been no infusion of human energy in the basement since last night, whereas Noa has spent the night in her room and has just recently left for school. It makes sense for us to hit the third floor first.

The team distributes recorders and equipment around Noa's living space. Pork, Beans and Satan are all fascinated by whatever it is they think we're doing. No sooner does Heather sit down on the couch than Satan is in her face, giving her all the love and demanding fuss in return.

"Did the disembodied footsteps happen again last night?" I ask. Heather shrugs.

"If they did, we all slept through them. It was a long day, and we were exhausted."

True indeed. Our team of investigators were so drained by the time we reached our respective accommodations that everyone was asleep almost as soon as our heads hit the pillow.

Now, we're raring to go.

Heather is first on deck for the headphones and blindfold. We have cameras recording video footage, audio recorders, an SLS camera running courtesy of Jill, and Tim taking notes as we ask questions. Heather is under for less than a minute when she opens with: *"Hello. Let's talk."*

We're off to the races.

"Perfect!" Tim beams. "That's why we're here."

"I'm here."

"How are you this morning?" Brad asks.

"Cool! What do you want?"

"We would love to just ask questions, and we'd appreciate it if you'd answer as best you can," Tim says. "If we knew your name, it would be easier to talk with you."

"Do it," Heather replies with emphasis. *"It's behind. It's behind."*

We all look at one another. Behind *who?* Behind *what?*

Beneath the hood, Heather hears the sound of a woman's laughter.

"Can you see us here?" Tim wants to know. Heather shakes her head.

"Not here. Not now."

Ping. I look at my tablet. The AI software has generated an image of a little girl wearing a dress. On the SLS camera, Jill is picking up what looks like a figure in the doorway of Noa's bedroom. I'm not convinced that this is paranormal. I've seen the SLS misinterpret tall vertical structures such as doorframes for human figures in the past. Still, Jill is keeping a close eye on it, to see if anything changes.

"Speak! Speak now!" Heather's tone is insistent. We'll learn later that there are four different voices, all speaking at the same time, all competing for her attention. There's another ping. The AI app shows a new picture, this one depicting four human beings standing in some kind of natural body of water.

Four.

"Ssshhh!" Heather snaps, then barks: *"Don't tell them!"*

Again with the secrecy.

"It's a problem!" Heather says, followed immediately by: *"I want to tell!"*

"You can tell us," Brad coaxes. "There's nothing anyone can do to you now."

"Ssshhh! I'm here." That's a male voice, according to Heather. She then hears a female voice insisting: *"Just stop. Stop!"*

There's an undeniably unfriendly vibe associated with some of these communications. It's hard to shake the feeling that somebody doesn't want a secret of some kind to come to light, and that someone else seems equally determined to share that secret with us.

"Go away! Stop! Don't! Stop!" This is followed by: *"She died here!"*

Who, we are all wondering, is she?

Tim entreats the communicator to give us a name or names to work with. He is ignored.

A child's voice breaks in with *"Hello!"* Immediately, an adult female responds with: *"Don't talk!"*

"Can you let the man speak, please?" Brad requests.

"NO!" Heather booms. *"No! Fuck off!"*

"Why won't you let him speak?" Rob wants to know.

"Don't do that!" Heather raises a hand and points directly at me. *"Stop! STOP!"*

I'm taking notes for what will ultimately become the book you're now reading. There's no way Heather could know where I'm sitting, because she had the blindfold in place before I sat down. I'm getting the impression that somebody really doesn't like the idea of me sharing this story with the world.

"Out! You!" She jabs her finger at me aggressively. *""Stop! Stop!"*

Then come the pleas for help.

"Go! Go! GET THE FUCK OUT!" Heather continues to point directly at me.

"Richard has permission to be here from the homeowners," Tim points out. "You don't own this home anymore." If they ever did, I muse, staring back at the blindfolded Heather, completely unfazed.

She reveals that she just heard three separate and distinct voices say the words: *Go away! Don't trust!* and *Stop!*

There are more cries for help.

"Jeff. It's cold."

"Is there any chance that Jeff is with us right now?" Tim asks.

"Who are you?"

"My name is Tim. I'm here with this group of people, trying to tell the story of this house—"

"Ssshhh! STOP!"

"You seem agitated," says Brad, playing Captain Obvious.

"Shush! Stop! STOP!" What comes next is intriguing. *"After eight. The family comes after eight!"*

Which family? Who and what are they talking about?

"Oh!" Heather yipes, jolting upright in her seat as though given an electric shock. *"Fuck!"*

She takes the headphones and blindfold off.

"It felt as if somebody got right up in my face," Heather explains, "and yelled *NO!* At the same time, someone slapped me hard on the back."

I don't blame her for getting out.

The ever-fearless Jill hot swaps with Heather. We tried this before, putting Brad in to sub for Heather, and now I want to see what happens when we replace one female with another.

"Help," is the first thing she hears, *"We're done."*

"Can you please speak to us a little more?" Brad requests. "We're trying to understand the family connection here."

"Who is the family that comes after eight?" I ask.

"Ssshhh," Jill responds. *"Let me think."*

Peering at the SLS screen, Rob says it looks as if somebody is peeking around the door frame. "You're welcome to come out here and join us."

"Rob," Jill says, her Estes voice softer and less excited than Heather's. There's no way she could have known that he would speak at that precise moment in time.

Her interactions are getting fewer and further between but are no less interesting for that. *"There's hope,"* she says. *"Him."*

"And who is that?" asks Tim. "Can you please give us a name or a description?"

"Ssshhh!" After a pause, she adds: *"Meet me in front."*

Heather asks for the names of whoever might be here. *"Get out,"* Jill says flatly.

"Do you want me to get out?" Heather seeks clarification.

"Something bothers me."

"What does?"

The answer is an emphatic *"Be silent."* Next comes: *"Bad man."*

"Do you know the name of the bad man?" asks Heather.

"Fuck." Jill swears in a flat, emotionless way. After a moment, she adds: *"He's gone."*

"He's left?" Heather asks.

"Yeah," Jill confirms.

Rob notes that the figure has disappeared from the SLS.

"Would you please meet us on the deck?" I ask. "Just you, and us. Nobody else."

"It's dark," Jill says.

"Meet us there, and we'll do our very best to help you," I promise.

The session tapers off. Finally, Jill removes the headphones and blindfold. Both her portion of the Estes Method and Heather's were plagued with resistance from one or more of the communicators, yet it also seems that at least one of them wants to try and tell us something.

Getting to my feet, I go over to the window and look outside. It's a cool, clear day. Outside the room, in the hallway, we're met by Satan, who has been patiently waiting for his mother to give him some fuss. Heather scratches behind his ears, eliciting a wag or two, then fetches herself a cardigan. We all make our way to the deck, and what we hope will be a rendezvous with one of the house's resident spirits.

No sooner do we reach the bottom of the staircase, than we start hearing the sound of footsteps following us down from the third floor. There's nobody up there; neither living human beings nor one of the three dogs. Hopefully, the steps are coming from whoever it is that's going to meet us out on the deck. They stop as quickly as they began.

There's a couch conveniently located on the back porch, which Heather sits down on and eagerly reaches for the Estes equipment. She's as determined as the rest of us to get to the bottom of the haunting. It's crisp but not too cold outdoors. This is the same deck on which the male apparition has been spotted on several occasions.

"Hi. Hello. We're here," Heather announces just seconds after slipping the headphones on.

Well, so much for having invited just one of them. It looks as if we're hosting a deck party.

"There's *ten* of us! I'm one of ten," she says.

"Can I get Seven of Nine?" I ask. I just can't help myself. It's a *Star Trek* in-joke.

"*Balls,*" Heather fires back. "*Why are you talking? Shush!*"
Indeed.

"*Give me space,*" she goes on, followed another "*Shush!*"

If there really are ten communicators present, this should be quite the night.

"Martin is here too."

"Hi, Martin," we chorus.

"Hey!"

Brad asks Martin whether there's something he'd like us to know.

"Door," Heather retorts. *"Close the door."*

I look over at the door. It is closed and has been since we first came out here.

A host *of stops, shushes,* and *help me* are interspersed with *"We're here"* and *"We all died."*

"When?" Brad wants to know.

He gets no answer. Some of the voices she's hearing are garbled. Others are crystal clear. Yet they're talking on top of one another in their eagerness to communicate, making it difficult for Heather to make sense of it all.

"Pregnant," she says, followed by: *"Happened here. It's here. Outside."*

I look around the fenced-in yard, curious as to what "it" might be. What happens next makes me think that the speaker might possibly be referring to a baby.

"It was mine. Mine, mine." She then adopts an accusatory tone. *"Come out. You! Come out. Get out. Ssshhh!"*

The session devolves into something of a word salad, as multiple communicators pile in on top of one another. Some are telling the others to shut up; the others are apparently trying to convey some sort of message.

It's become an exercise in frustration.

A light breeze ruffles Heather's hair. She can hear the sound of somebody crying, saying that they're sorry, and repeatedly begging for someone to *"please stop!"*

"Sorry for what?" Brad asks gently.

"Evil. Around her now."

Apropos of nothing, the SLS camera shuts down. Jill is surprised. She hasn't switched it off. Someone else apparently has.

"I don't like you," Heather says, her brow furrowing. *"No. Daniel. Shush."*

Daniel, of course, is one of the former residents of the property.

"I don't like you," she repeats, followed by: *"Whore! Go!I lived here!"*

More shushing comes next.

"Hurt. Accident." Heather jabs a finger at me again. I'm six feet away from her, and yet she seems to know exactly where I'm standing. *"Go away! Out!"*

"Did the accident occur here at the house?" Brad asks, trying to get things back on track.

"Get out! Ssshhh! YOU! Ssshhh! Liar! Liar!"

Although Heather herself is calm, the communicators are growing increasingly angry. Now seems like a good time to hot swap another investigator with her. Brad volunteers, and in a few seconds he and Heather have traded places.

"All of them, here," he begins.

"Why will you not let us speak with just one person?" Tim demands. "What are you hiding?"

"Rich," is the reply. Whether this is meant to be my own nickname, or an indicator that somebody has a lot of money, is unclear. From behind us, just inside the house, there's an eruption of loud barking. Peeking around the window, we can't see anybody that would have caused the dogs to become agitated.

"Are we speaking with Rich now?" Tim enquires.

"Evil," comes the reply. *"We're gone."*

Brad's hearing a man and a woman talking over one another. His face is a mask of concentration as he tries to sort out one voice from the other. He gets a name — Esther — but most of what Brad's hearing seems choppy and difficult to comprehend. Single words, such as *"fear,"* are difficult to contextualize without more information. At least he's not getting shushed, as Heather consistently has been.

"That's it," signals the end of Brad's session. All communication stops, as though an off switch has been flipped. We give it a minute, just to make sure, and then bring him out.

"There was a female voice and a male voice," he tells us. "They were arguing in the background, and it was too garbled to make out a lot of what they said. Yesterday, it sounded to me that the male voice was trying to dominate things. Today, it seemed like the two of them were on more equal ground."

"I got the vibe of two siblings bickering," Heather adds as we police up our equipment and go back inside the house.

Jill is still puzzled at the behavior of her SLS, which contrived to shut itself down repeatedly over the space of several minutes. However, the app has done that before at other locations, so I'm inclined to ascribe that to the equipment itself, not to the paranormal.

As we gather around the kitchen table for tea and coffee, I'm pondering the numbers game. During the Estes session in Noa's living space, four distinct voices were heard talking. The AI app also conjured up an image of four figures in a pond or lake. Out here on the back porch, Heather clearly stated that there were "ten of us."

Prompted by the ever-astute Rob, I'm now doing the math. Four spirit communicators...footsteps following us down the stairs...I look around. Me, Heather, Rob, Brad, Tim, and Jill...that makes six. Six living people. Four dead.

A total of ten.

Coincidence — or something far stranger?

Heather points out that the woman's voice sounded different to the one she has heard calling out "*hello*" inside the house. Could one of the two women perhaps be the Lady in Blue?

So far, we've been assuming that *we*— Heather, Brad, myself — are the ones being shushed. Yet it's equally likely that one of the communicators is trying to keep certain things quiet. What I'm certain about is those occasions in which a blindfolded Heather was trying to shut *me* up, pointing an accusatory finger right at me. That seems very clear cut.

Every house has its secrets, not all of them pleasant. Why should this one be any different?

Chapter Eighteen

Arryn's Adult Beverages - Lady Marmalade

L *ady Marmalade*

1. 1.5 oz Maker's Mark (or any good bourbon you have lying around)

2. 0.25 oz Jameson Whiskey (I ran out of bourbon one day and topped up with Jameson as it was all I had, now it's a staple of the drink)

3. Bar spoon Grand Marnier

4. 0.25 oz Fresh squeezed mandarin orange juice

5. 2-3 drops Angostura bitters

6. Heaped teaspoon T&T Korean Honey Citron Tea

7. Add all ingredients to a large shaker full of ice and shake

8.   Get your chilled rocks glasses ready for service by adding a teaspoon of T&T Korean Honey Citron Tea to the bottom, before adding a fancy oversized ice cube on top

9.   Strain your cocktail over the ice cube slowly so as not to disturb the marmalade

10.   Garnish with a dehydrated round of mandarin orange (we got a cheap countertop dehydrator and make our own garnishes, it's super economical)

11.   Drink while you consider all the other drinks you can make with jams and preserves...such a better use than spreading them on toast

Chapter Nineteen

"Hail, Satan!"

Up to this point in our investigation, we haven't kept Raff informed of our findings. Now, he's taking a break in the middle of his working day in order to pitch in and experience things for himself.

I've always believed that skeptics get a bad rap. Barring those who lean toward extreme skepticism (flatly refusing to seriously consider *anything* that is presented to them as being potentially paranormal) I have always believed that honest, open-minded skeptics are the paranormal investigator's best friend. Nobody plays Devil's Advocate better. Their insights can often skewer theories that, on closer examination, would not bear up under serious scrutiny.

Raff is an intelligent and educated young man, and we're really looking forward to getting his take on the haunting of his family home.

"I'm open to the possibility that there are things we can't see, such as ghosts or whatever," he explains. "I've never experienced anything that I'd consider paranormal here. There are bats in the house. Squirrels. Three dogs...so hearing noises isn't something I'd automatically attribute to the otherworldly."

That sounds entirely fair and balanced to me.

"Mom, Dad, and Noa have all heard voices in the house, and my sister has heard those footsteps," he recalls, "but nothing like that has ever happened to me."

The same holds true for Doc, and for the friends and associates they've brought into the house during their time.

"There's the occasional time when I'm brushing my teeth at one in the morning, and it feels a little bit eerie," Doc reveals. "I never had that in my home in Toronto, and I never get uncomfortable in places. It happens in the hall outside the Speakeasy. But I've never had any issues, no trouble sleeping."

I appreciate their candor. Feeling creeped out in an old funeral home is an entirely normal response, we can all agree. The only possible exception was a four-week stretch when the Blumbergs were out of town, and Doc was all alone in the funeral home, dog sitting. Like any decent human, he allowed the dogs to sleep in the same room as him. At that time, his bedroom was what is now the gym.

All three dogs were agitated every night without fail, growling and barking at something unseen. However, playing Devil's Advocate, it's worth pointing out that for the dogs, the status quo had been interrupted. Their family was gone. It makes complete sense that they would have become agitated.

We give Raff a quick overview of the Estes Method. He's quick on the uptake and after a couple of minutes, Raff is ready to dive in.

To kick things off, we start in the living room, which hasn't played a significant part in our investigation thus far. He makes himself comfortable on the couch, sitting slightly forward with his forearms resting just above his knees. On goes the blindfold, and then the headphones.

The sweep rate and other settings remain the same ones we've used for the past few days. The only variable we're changing for this session is the identity of the listener, and the part of the house in which he is listening.

"I hear a man's voice," he begins tentatively, concentrating as hard as he can. "A lot of what seems to be just radio talk."

That's exactly what he's hearing, as the scanner slips its way between commercial radio stations.

There's a low, menacing growl. Beans has just raised his head, ears perking up, and is staring intently toward a corner of the room.

"Some vague mumbling," Raff notes.

Tim and I are both poised ready to take notes.

"There's a woman's voice in between the radio stations...can you speak more clearly, please?"

After a moment, Heather asks whether the unseen communicators find Raff annoying. She flashes an impish grin.

"There she is again," Raff notes. He's not hearing any clear words at all. "There's definitely a very softly spoken female voice in there."

"This might be your only opportunity to talk with Raff in this way," I point out, talking to what seems like thin air. "Surely there's something you'd like to say to him?"

"You can start out with something as simple as a hello or a hi," Tim encourages.

"Definitely some muttering," Raff pulls the headphones a little tighter over his ears. "Sounded like a man that time."

Beyond that, however, there's nothing. No intelligible speech. Raff tries it for ten minutes and then we bring him out. It was a very professional and open-minded attempt.

"That feels very strange," he says, coming back out into daylight. "That muttering wasn't you guys, and it definitely wasn't radio either. The first couple of mutterings were female. The last one was deeper, it sounded like a guy."

For his first ever attempt at the Estes Method, it was a valiant effort. His friend and business partner, Doc, is next up on deck. He's new to the technique too. We keep the same settings. He's sitting a couple of seats down from Raff, and it takes just a minute to get him under the hood.

At first, he's not hearing anything other than the radio. After a couple of minutes, he hears a female voice, though he can't make out exactly what it was saying — if there were even words at all. Seconds later, it happens again.

"It's like a weird groan," Doc laughs. "It's quick. Then it's gone. Still no words."

A bass, rhythmic sound makes us all look down at the floor. Satan is snoring up a storm, like a chainsaw going to work in a forest.

"Sounded like the word *'sleep,'* and it definitely wasn't a man's voice," Doc says. That's interesting; Satan is most definitely, very loudly asleep. The timing of the word is very apropos.

"We could all leave and go to lunch," Brad smirks, clearly kidding. "Leave him under for a bit."

"Or we could *not* be dicks," I point out.

"What did you mean by the word *sleep?*" Tim asks.

"Five," Doc says. "That's the clearest one so far. A girl said the word *five."*

It's worth noting that, according to the timer we have running, there's just five minutes left in Doc's Estes session.

"It's gone quiet," he tells us. "Just the flickering of the channels."

When the five minutes are up, we bring him out. He's intrigued by what happened. His results were a little clearer than Raff's. Neither of their sessions was on a par with those of Heather or Brad. Of course, neither Heather nor Brad have done an Estes in this part of the house yet.

"Very interesting," Doc smiles, "and very creepy."

The team observes that it's starting to feel quiet, less energetic. Stephen and Jill are gone — they're on a side quest to get tattoos. This is the same time as yesterday that the energy levels in the house seem to have declined.

It's time for a lunch break. While the team and I are enjoying the culinary delights of Dresden, why don't you, Dear Reader, consider making one of Arryn's liquid delights? Enjoy it responsibly, of course, and let's meet back here in a few minutes to continue our journey.

As we're finishing our late lunch and strolling back toward the Blumberg place, it appears that we've somehow managed to anger Thor the God of Thunder. Lightning flashes across the afternoon sky. Thunder rumbles right on its heels, only slightly louder than the deep snores of contentment made by Satan during our EVP session.

Murphy's Law being a thing, we're halfway home when we're pelted with hailstones. We break into something halfway between a run and a lope, shielding our heads with our hands, in a vain attempt to ward off the bombardment of solidified ice that is rattling off the roofs and threatening parked cars for miles around.

On the plus side, by the time we rock up to the front door of the funeral home and pound on the glass for Arryn to let us in, I get to make what might be my favorite dad joke of the entire trip.

The bearded one lets us in. We stampede through the front door, right into the slavering maws of the canine welcoming committee. Sounding entirely too pleased with myself, I look the Prince of Dogginess in the eye and boom out: "Hail, Satan!"

If looks could kill, I'd have more daggers in my back than Julius Caesar right now.

Once we've dried off, it's time to launch into the next phase of our investigation, reasoning that there's no time like the present — and no ambience like that of a thunderstorm — to try and make a deeper connection with the spirits of the former funeral home.

Our target: the Pink Room. Now that the school day is over, Noa is eager to try the Estes Method for herself. Rob coaches her on what to expect, while her mother keeps a watchful eye on things from the corner of the room.

The Pink Room is located on the ground floor, at the back of the house. It directly abuts the deck on which the earlier EVP session took place. Noa sits in a corner of the plush couch, propped up on a small mountain of pillows. Pork and Beans take up guard positions protectively at Noa's feet, like a pair of sentries who don't want to let anybody near their human.

Rob films the session, while the rest of us set out recorders and find comfortable seating on the floor, in chairs, or leaning against the walls.

"Somebody must want to talk to Noa," Heather declares. "I mean, you sit right there on her bed..."

All we can hear is the muted swish of the spirit box as it hops from station to station.

"We've given you some alone time, and now we're back," says Tim. "We're here for the evening and we'd love to talk with you again."

Aside from breathing, Noa barely moves. A clickety-clack of nails on uncarpeted floor heralds the manifestation of a panting Satan, who enters the room and plops down on the floor with a hefty thud.

"Do you know who has been opening and closing Noa's bedroom door?" Heather wants to know.

Outside in the hallway, there is suddenly footsteps. Tim peeks out. They stop. Nobody is there. All of the dogs are accounted for. Arryn is working in his office at the front of the house. Doc and Raff are downstairs in the basement.

"Who's walking around out there in the hallway?" Rob calls out.

There's no reply. None whatsoever.

Now it's Pork's turn to look up and growl at something the rest of us can't see.

Almost fifteen minutes have passed so far, and Noa hasn't gotten anything. After a brief consultation, we agree to swap Heather for her daughter. Rob carefully brings her out from under, taking the headphones and blindfold. Interestingly, Noa reveals that something physically tapped on her headphones several times while she was under the hood.

Of voices, there were none.

"Rich," is the first word out of Heather's mouth. *"Speak. I've got nothing really to say. Ssshhh!"*

Already, I'm of the opinion that she's hearing multiple different communicators speaking to one another, going back and forth.

"Are you trying to have Rich speak with us right now?" Tim asks. He is aggressively shushed.

"Dance," Heather says, telling us that she's hearing what sounds like a man and a woman bickering. Rob asks her communicator whether, if they used to dance, which floor of the house they did it on. The response is immediate. *"Three."*

Color us all impressed. The third floor is indeed where dancing and social functions are said to have taken place. The answer was spot on.

"We were together," Heather continues.

"How long?"

"All night."

That raises eyebrows. Rob asks their names, and is given the name *Ed.*

"Is that short for Edward?"

"Yes! Eddie, and..."

"What's the other name?" Rob prompts, encouragingly.

"Anne or Eva," Heather responds.

"It's nice to meet you two."

"Edward and Anne or Eva," mutters Tim, writing them down. Again, he is aggressively shushed.

"We're local," Heather goes on. *"From here. Anne. There's room for all of us."*

If they're talking about the house, there is indeed room for a great many people, whether alive or dead.

"There was a stage...men stayed over," she continues. *"...and women..."*

"So, you're saying there was a women's parlor?" Rob is slightly confused.

"No," is the firm reply. "There's a man speaking, but I can't understand him."

This last was delivered in Heather's normal speaking voice. It is followed by a return to her Estes tone: *"They won't let me. Family."*

"Was this a family room?" Rob asks.

"Ssshhh! Not you."

"Are you shushing me or someone else?"

Satan growls for no apparent reason, staring toward the empty doorway and the hall beyond.

"Who do you keep shushing?" Rob wants to know.

"Her."

"Who's her?"

"HEATHER. Shush!"

So, there we have it. Somebody wants Heather to keep quiet.

"Don't want to talk," she blurts out. *"Stop! Lowlife! Shush! Speaking is done! Silence! Silent. We're all done!"*

Rob tries to make an accommodation, but all he gets is *"DONE!"*

"They hate me," Heather shakes her head ruefully.

Noa's been quietly watching the whole thing. Her verdict on the Estes Method is a simple: "Cool."

While we're waiting for our guest investigators to arrive, we follow Heather up to the third floor so that she can Estes again in Noa's living space. This part of the funeral home has been fairly chatty so far, and we're all looking forward to seeing what it might say to the lady of the house.

Taking a seat on the couch, Heather pops on the headphones and blindfold without prompting and goes back under for another session. Same box, same settings.

"Is Susan up here with us?" Brad asks, hoping for more information on the name that he both heard and captured as an EVP.

There's no response. Heather sits quietly, slowly breathing and sinking into the couch.

"Who just shushed Heather?" Stephen wants to know.

"You," she says after a moment. *"Ssshhh! Stop!"*

We all chuckle. Again with the shushing. She points to her shoulders, letting us know that she again feels a pair of hands pushing down on her from above and behind. Nobody is standing at the back of the couch...

...nobody that we can see, anyway.

There's a low growl. At first, I think it's one of the dogs, but a sheepish Stephen confesses to it being his stomach. It's giving Pork, Beans, and Satan a run for their money.

"A man's voice just said *stop*," Heather announces.

"Are you the same people from downstairs?"

Heather slaps at her left knee, adding that somebody is touching her leg. Then she hears a young child crying. As a mother, that has to be saddening.

"Steve!" she insists. *"Steve!"*

"Is this anybody we've already spoken to, either like this or using another method of communication?" Stephen asks.

The response comes in the form of a male voice, which is pitched too low for Heather to make out.

"Can you be a little—" Stephen begins. He is cut off with another vehement *"Ssshhh!"*

"...clearer?"

"Man's voice. Can't understand it."

"Typical man," Stephen deadpans, earning himself a blend of chuckles, eye rolls...and another *Ssshhh!*

"It's okay to speak," says Stephen. "Be as chatty as you want."

"Hi!" This is a new communicator, one that seems happier and peppier, based on Heather's tone. But just as quickly, we're back to *"Ssshhh!!!"*

"Hello," Stephen amiably greets the new arrival. "Please be aware that nobody on either this side or the other has any right to shut you up. There are no restrictions on who you can talk to or what you can say."

"Wait!" Heather hisses forcefully. *"Ssshhh! SSSHHH!!!"*

Somebody *really* doesn't want this communicator talking to us, it seems.

"Stop! STOP!"

"Why?" Stephen asks, his tone laconic.

The team is also using an SLS, a Structured Light Sensing camera, to scan the room. One of the more controversial devices in the paranormal field, this gadget throws out a blizzard of infrared light, then attempts to analyze the scatter. If the IR light hits something solid, the SLS will sometimes interpret that as being a figure, most likely humanoid in build. The problem is that these cameras are best employed on tripods for maximum stability. When moved around, particularly if hand-held, they tend to be more prone to false positives. Some paranormal investigators love the SLS camera. Others disavow it completely. I'm on the fence (I've been impressed with its results on a handful of occasions, always when it was statically mounted) but lean slightly more toward the naysayers' camp than that of the believers. Each to their own.

According to the SLS output, it looks as if some kind of figure is being picked up in the doorway to Noa's bedroom.

"Can you tell us who that is in the doorway?" Tim calls out.

After a minute, Heather says *"No!"* It's followed by yet another *"Ssshhh!"*

On the screen, a second figure appears alongside the first. It's smaller, almost child-sized by comparison to the original.

"LET'S GO!" Heather all but shouts. Then she hears the sound of laughter.

Checking the time, I note that Heather has been under the hood for a while. I want to bring her out, but also don't want to waste the momentum we've already gotten going. Brad volunteers to do a hot swap, the idea being that we'll take the headphones and blindfold off Heather and immediately do a switcheroo, putting them on him without anybody taking a break. I'm intrigued to know whether he's going to be subject to the same kind of shushing and physical touches that Heather has been dealing with so far.

"Woman's voice," Brad announces almost instantly.

"Can you tell us more about Susan?" Tim requests.

"Hurt."

"Susan was hurt?" Tim leans forward, ready to scribe down some notes.

"Her mother," Brad goes on, and then comes the now-familiar *Ssshhh!*

So, it isn't just Heather that somebody in this house wants to silence. Brad's getting the same treatment too.

Ssshhh! More forceful this time. Clearly, we're angering somebody. Under these circumstances, I'm okay with that.

"It's coming," he adds. *"Him."*

"Who is him?" I want to know. "Or, more accurately, who is he?"

Brad tells us that he's hearing a man's voice, but it's too garbled for him to make out any of the words.

There's suddenly a sound like a very sad werewolf sobbing its heart out. All eyes turn to look at Stephen — his stomach, to be precise. He has the wherewithal to look slightly embarrassed as the ghost of his dinner resurfaces to haunt us all.

"Did you enjoy talking with me earlier?" Heather asks. "Did I upset you?"

"YOU." Brad's tone is suddenly full of sullen menace.

"Is there a reason you want me quiet?"

"You need to go."

"Why do I need to go?"

SSSHHH!

"Why do I need to shush?" Heather holds her ground.

"It's her house," I point out. "She owns this place. Not you."

"You have a big mouth," Brad drawls back.

"Do you like being in Noa's room?" Heather wants to know. For her trouble, she gets shushed again.

"They're coming...them." Brad adds that he hears a growl, and then the word *"Lies."*

"Why are you so defensive?" Stephen interjects.

"What are you talking about?" Brad's communicator is having none of it, dismissing the priest's concern. *"Bitch, stop."*

Unfazed, Heather demands to know the identity of "the bitch."

"That's it." There's a finally to Brad's tone that suggests he's over and done with this conversation.

"Are we done?" Stephen seeks clarification.

"Yes," Brad fires back. His voice is monotone and deadpan. Removing the equipment, he recalls hearing a "deep, baritone male voice, garbled." Heather's nodding. That tracks with what she heard also. The same communicator was apparently trying to shut them both up, for reasons best known only to them.

"This guy was trying to talk, but the words weren't coming out quite right," he adds.

Something else they both heard: either a child or a young woman whimpering in distress. That, to my mind at least, is far more concerning than the dominant male who's trying to throw his weight around. However, as we talk it over, I realize that I might have leapt to an assumption here. Heather felt as though the male was doing the shushing. Brad, on the other hand, got the impression that the same man was being shushed by the woman. The shushing had a feminine quality to it, in his view.

The question remains...who is this secretive lady, and what does she have to hide?

Chapter Twenty

Arryn's Adult Beverages - Lavendar Haze

L **avender Haze**
   1. *1 oz Tanqueray Gin*

   2. *0.25 oz Grey Goose Le Citron Vodka*

   3. *0.25 oz Rossi D'Asiago Limoncello*

   4. *0.5 oz Fresh squeezed lemon juice (use Meyer lemons if you can get them)*

   5. *0.5 oz Lavender simple syrup*

   This is a quick and easy syrup to make

   Add 1 cup water to ¾ cup white granulated sugar, with ¼ cup honey, to a pot

   Put over a low heat, you don't want to boil anything just dissolve the sugar and honey

   Add 6-10 fresh lavender blossoms to the pot as it warms

I add a small dash of purple food coloring to the water, but this is just for the look of it, if you don't have then you can skip this step

Once everything has dissolved and warmed through, extracting the lavender oils should only take 5 min at most. Turn off the heat, remove from the burner and let the mixture cool

After its cooled strain into a container

6.   Add all the ingredients to a glass cocktail mixing jug full of ice and stir well

7.   Strain into a chilled Nick & Nora glass, ideally vintage or antique

8.   Top with a good splash of dry prosecco (I use Ruffino)

9.   Garnish with a fresh lavender flower

10.   Drink knowing you've created a great alternative to that afternoon cup of tea

Chapter Twenty-One

Pauly and the Weirdos

J ill is off doing her own thing, and Stephen is scrying in the Speakeasy (a time-honored tradition of using a mirror to attempt communication with the Spirit World) so the rest of us head over to the gym to investigate it for the first time. Later tonight, we'll change tactics and do something other than the Estes Method, but for now, I want to see whether the spirits will talk to us via the radio here.

This time out, Tim is going under the hood. Rob videos the session while Brad is acting as scribe, taking notes and asking questions. Once we find somewhere to sit, it takes no time at all to get the session rolling.

"Contact," is Tim's opener.

"Hello," Rob and I greet the communicator. Brad's greeting is a rather creepily whispered *"Hi."*

"Who's there?" Tim asks. Brad introduces us one by one and asks who's talking.

"David."

We say hello to David by name and ask him whether this is his space.

"Richard, help," says Tim. Is David asking for help, I wonder, or offering to help? The syntax can be read either way, particularly with Tim's characteristically flat, level delivery of Estes results.

"How can I help?" I ask.

"In charge." Although we're a team of equals, I am responsible for coordinating this trip and bringing it all together.

"I'm hearing a male voice," Tim announces for clarification. The man in question starts asking for help. He gives us the name *Rick*, followed by: *"That's weird,"* and the sound of a male laughing.

A female voice breaks in and says the word *"Iowa."* That's where Rob hails from. "Hello?" he says questioningly.

"Hello," Tim echoes.

"How can I help you?"

"I'm here."

Maybe so, but that doesn't shed any light on how we can be of help.

"Where are you from?" Rob asks.

"Canada. East."

"This area?" Brad puts in. "Dresden?"

Tim shakes his head. *"All over."*

"Have you been to Iowa?"

"Yes."

Brad leans forward. "What was your occupation?"

It's starting to sound like one of the weirdest job interviews ever.

"Voices all around me," says Tim, shaking his head.

Unfortunately, what we get doesn't make a whole lot of sense at first. When asked which floor they're on, Tim comes back with *"Seven."* Clearly, that's impossible. There isn't a building in Dresden with seven floors.

Rob is making a little too much noise, rearranging some of his equipment. For his sins, he is told to "fuck off." Once again, a profane communicator is with us.

Things get a little more interesting when Brad addresses the rumor of there being some kind of journal containing personal secrets hidden somewhere within the walls of the house. Do the spirits know anything about it?

"Nope," Tim says flatly.

The remainder of the conversation becomes similarly dismissive. It seems that whoever is talking to Tim really doesn't want to cooperate with our quest for answer. That has been a theme throughout our time here.

Just in case it's the listener, Rob swaps with Tim. "Hey," he begins, the moment he puts on the headphones.

It's quiet for the next few minutes. Rob is getting shushed, even when he isn't actually speaking.

"Is someone trying to keep these secrets hidden?" Brad asks.

"There's a woman's voice, but I can't make out the words," Rob frowns, screwing up his face in concentration.

"Rich" comes up again, something we've heard before in other parts of the house. We're still not sure whether it's a name or a description of somebody's financial status. Next comes *"Liar"* and *"Out,"* which Rob says were delivered in a very creepy voice.

What is it, I wonder aloud, that needs to be kept secret. Rob hears a little girl say the word: *"Evil."*

"Hiding," comes next. Brad asks what was hiding — a person, perhaps, or possibly an object? The response is a most unhelpful *"Yes."*

A minute passes. Rob seems startled. He announces that somebody just shoved the back of his chair — hard. "I know that wasn't any of you guys," he says, trusting us completely. He's right. Nobody is within touching distance of him, let alone behind him.

"Dead," Rob says, and when we attempt to ask another question, we're told to "get lost."

The conversation — if conversation it truly is — deteriorates into yet another jumble of apparently meaningless word salad. It's getting frustrating. We can all feel it.

As we get together to plan our next move, my mind is preoccupied with investigative methodology. I'm well aware that we have leaned heavily on the Estes Method so far, not least because it has given us a chance to involve three out of the four Blumbergs directly. I want to try something new, but first, Brad has a hankering to do one last Estes session for the day...this time, in the Speakeasy.

It's just a few steps away, so we're ensconced within the comfy chairs of the Speakeasy in less than five minutes. No sooner has he put the headphones in place than Brad is hearing a male voice talking. Right out of the gate, he's getting shushed. That's par for the course in this house, and words are still coming through despite the clear desire somebody is showing to shut us up.

The downside is, none of those words seem particularly relevant or meaningful. A female voice, very faint but almost certainly adult, begins talking on the periphery of Brad's hearing. Try as he might, he can't make out anything that she's saying. Ten minutes in, and it's shaping up to be the quietest EVP session we've done so far, with the possible exception of Raff's debut effort earlier.

Just as we're about to give it up, a communicator named Rick introduces himself. *"Poor boy,"* he says, though whether he's referring to himself or somebody else is unclear. *"Fucked up."*

"On what, or how?" I ask.

"Ssshhh!"

I roll my eyes. Not this again. Always there is secrecy inside this house.

Somewhat more ominously, we get *"Payback."*

"Payback for what?"

"Glass eye."

Rob and I share a look. That's really specific. Morticians sometimes use glass eyes in certain cases while they are preparing a body for a viewing. Our attempts to gather more information are stymied by yet more shushing.

Some of what comes next has a definite 1960s/1970s vibe; phrases like *"far out"* and *"my pad"* have largely fallen out of use by now. Is Brad hearing the voice of someone who died half a century ago?

After the session trickles away into nothingness, we bring him out. Stifling a yawn, he stretches, the red glow of the Speakeasy light glinting from his bald pate. "Words would start coming through, then they'd be gone," he tells us. "I got the impression that somebody was trying to talk but kept getting cut off."

Whoever wants to shush us seems to be succeeding.

It's time to change our tactics — but first, we need to check in with our special guests...

...a pair of certified weirdos, and a dog.

John EL Tenney is as knowledgeable as he is difficult to get in contact with. A seasoned researcher of all things weird and wonderful with decades of experience, he co-hosts the *What's Up, Weirdo?* podcast with Jessica Knapik, a tattoo artist who is passionate about Mixed

Martial Arts (MMA), a broad range of TV shows and movies, especially true crime documentaries. She has a near-encyclopedic knowledge of popular culture and serial killers...and the actor Billy Zane. She also knows a thing or two about ghosts.

Tenney is like that weird uncle you have that makes Christmas and Thanksgiving so much fun. Think of Jessica as the fun aunt that helps keep him grounded in the real world and uses the word "fuck" in sentences like most people use punctuation.

Don't mistake them for being a couple. They're best friends, and the *real* brains of the operation would be Jessica's dog, Toad. He's secretly the one calling all the shots.

"The Blumbergs only have two rules," I tell John and Jessica as they climb the stairs to the main floor, Toad happily panting along behind them. "First, no smoking within a mile of the house. Two, no saying the F-word."

"We should probably turn around and fuckin' leave," Jessica deadpans. It's an open secret in the paranormal field that the best way to talk with Tenney is to catch him on one of his numerous smoke breaks.

I'm glad they're both here. Getting two extra perspectives on this location is going to be valuable, especially when it comes from people with opinions we respect.

Although both Toad and the three Blumberg dogs are well-behaved, in order to prevent any accidental outbursts of excessive canine enthusiasm, Heather and Arryn have consigned Pork, Beans and Satan behind closed doors for a while. This allows Jessica, Toad and Tenney to have free rein to explore the house in their own inimitable style.

Arryn, John, Jessica, Heather,
and Toad.

First, however, there are introductions to be made. Everyone's getting along like a house on fire from the outset. Like us, the terrible trio has driven across the border from Detroit into Canada. Along the way, they've gone shopping for cool books.

Chatting with Tenney, I share a local newspaper clipping from *The Windsor Star* dating back to Saturday 9 November 1957. Titled *Farmers reveals visit of earlier "Sputnik"*, the article details how a Dresden farmer saw what he believed was a flying saucer one night in the late 1940s. The 35-foot-wide UFO, which had a red light on top of it, rose out of a field, buzzed the incredulous Dresdenite and his companion, then shot upward and disappeared into the heavens.

I bring it up because if there's such a thing as an expert on UFOs/UAPs/whatever we're calling them these days, then Tenney certainly qualifies. He isn't remotely surprised by the story, because he's familiar with this part of the country. From a UFOlogical perspective, it's saddening that many of the UFO and ghost stories which arose from this part of the province were arrogantly dismissed because they came from eyewitnesses of African descent. Coming as a surprise to absolutely nobody, bigotry, racism and xenophobia have always been a thing in paranormal/UFO interest circles, and disappointingly, they remain so to this day.

"We can assume that there are many more stories like this around Dresden that have gotten lost because people just didn't want to talk about them," Tenney concludes with an appropriately grave mien.

John, Jessica, the Blumbergs and my team spend the next half hour shooting the breeze. Heather sets down a bowl of water for Toad. With the ice well and truly broken, the newest additions to our team get the grand tour from Heather and Arryn.

She and Tenney are about to spend some time investigating by themselves, hitting the laundry room and the master bathroom.

By mutual agreement, we're Estes'd out. We've been itching to try the Ouija board here, and Heather is keen to give it a try herself. Taking one of my travel boards out of my suitcase, I tuck it under one arm and start to head for the basement stairs.

Inspiration strikes.

"Arryn?"

"Hmmm?" He's pottering around the kitchen, getting together the necessary culinary equipment and ingredients for dinner. I tear a sheet of paper out of my notebook and set it down on the continent — I mean, the island. A pen goes next to it.

"Do me a favor, mate. As soon as we are all out of the room, write a number between one and a hundred on this bit of paper, would you?"

"Uh, sure." Arryn seems a little puzzled, but three days into the investigation, he's fast growing accustomed to our weird and quirky ways. "Then what do you want me to do with it?"

"Leave it right there, face up, on the kitchen counter."

Heather leads us down to the Speakeasy. I'm tail end Charlie, closing doors behind me as we go. None of us, me included, have seen what Arryn has just written on that piece of paper.

My reason for having him do so will soon be revealed to my friends. The board is circular, shaped that way by my friends at Death

State Paranormal, who hand craft each one. It's inlaid with the distinctive red and orange pattern of the Overlook Hotel carpet from Stanley Kubrick's movie version of *The Shining* by Stephen King.

We're accompanied by Heather's ever-present pair of bodyguards, Pork and Beans (Satan apparently has something better to do with his time) who flop down huffily onto the rugs which cover the floor.

Jill, Heather and Stephen are the first three participants. Each pulls up their high-backed chair to within comfortable reach of the table, in the center of the room. There's room for a fourth. Tim obliges, completing the circle.

Brad, Rob and I sit back and observe, taking notes and asking questions. The participants move the pointer, known more properly as the planchette, in a figure eight pattern around the board.

"I now open this board, but only for good spirits," Stephen begins. "No evil, no negativity is permitted to come through it. Only direct answers. No games. No players. Only honest and true forms of communication."

Stephen then invites communicators to work through the board to talk with us, letting us know when they're ready to talk. The planchette slides across the board, its tip resting on *Yes*.

So far, so good.

What comes next is a string of nonsensical letters and numbers; less a meaningful word or phrase, and more the kind of secure password that your Apple IOS might dream up in an attempt to foil hackers.

Stephen asks the communicator to spell out their name. GXES is hardly an encouraging start, but that's what we get. The planchette trails off listlessly. After a moment, Tim hops off and Noa jumps in, hopefully injecting a big bolus of teenager energy into the mix. Perhaps the spirits can make better use of it.

The planchette moves immediately to *Yes* and then, on request, back to the center of the board, making a low scraping sound as it does so. This time, the board gives its name as a more understandable *Pauly*.

"Pauly, have you ever lived in this house?" Heather asks.

No, the planchette responds, before returning to the center.

"Did you attend a funeral here?" Jill wants to know. The answer is a very strong, swift *Yes.*

Pauly claims that she is a woman, and, if the board is to be believed, the funeral was that of her husband. What year was that? The planchette jumps from one number to the next, in the sequence *1-9-4-7.*

"Pauly, how old was your husband?" Jill asks gently. The board gives the answer *84.*

"Was he from this area?" Stephen wants to know. "From Dresden?"

Yes again. *Guy* was apparently his name.

Pauly and Guy, from Dresden.

We're also given their surname, though I will not include it in this book, out of respect for living family members — because Pauly claims that they had children.

I clear my throat.

"Pauly, I'd like to ask you a favor please." The participants all shoot me a puzzled look, not knowing what I'm about to request. "Would you mind popping upstairs to the kitchen, where the nice man with the beard has written a number on a piece of paper? Please read that number, then come back and tell us what it is."

There is a delay of around five seconds, then the planchette is moving. It swoops confidently across the board to land on 8, then hops across to its neighbor, 7, then back to 8.

87 or 78?

"Is 87 the number, Pauly?" I ask for clarification. *Yes,* comes the reply. It's the strongest, most forceful movement yet.

"Thank you," Heather says. My phone is out, and I'm already texting Arryn.

WHAT'S THE NUMBER YOU WROTE, SIR?

There's a momentary pause. My phone vibrates.

It's a photograph of a piece of paper with the number 78 written on it.

The planchette has stopped moving. They're all looking at me expectantly.

I tell them the number.

The digits are the same; an 8 and a 7. Part of me thinks that they're so close to the actual number, it could easily be explained away as a minor mix-up. How many times have you remembered a number, such a street address or a phone number, the wrong way round? My fifty-year-old brain does it all the time, transposing numbers every time two-factor authentication sends me a security code.

On the other hand, the logical, skeptical part of my brain is screaming at me about bias. There's a one percent chance that the planchette, if it is being subconsciously manipulated by the participants, would guess the right number. That leaves a 99% likelihood of failure. Am I so emotionally invested in the haunting of the Blumberg house that my brain is willing to shunt aside the cold, hard math of the matter, and give the *"hey, maybe these are the right figures, just accidentally mixed up"* argument a free pass?

I just don't know...

...which means I should err on the side of skepticism.

What happens next is harder to explain, however. Prior to my coming out here, I was contacted by psychic medium and good friend MJ Dickson. She lives in the UK, and over the past year, she and I have conducted a number of remote mediumship experiments in which MJ tries to "tune in" to whichever location I am currently at, to see what she can pick up on. There are misses, but some of her psychic hits are so accurate, it borders on the uncanny.

I received a text message from her earlier in the day, stating a person's name. I won't reveal that name here, because that person may well still be alive and living locally. Stephen asks Pauly for the name of her children. The first name that the planchette spells out is exactly the same as the word MJ picked up psychically.

Coincidence? Conceivably.

Is the *87/78* a coincidence? Again, conceivably.

All of which raises the question: at what point do we stop believing in coincidence, and ascribe these answers to some kind of paranormal force or intelligence?

I don't know the answer for sure. I think that each and every one of us sets that bar differently than others. Speaking only for myself, I'm fast losing the ability to think that what's happening in this house is purely coincidental.

"Pauly, do you watch over the new family that lives here?" Rob asks. The answer is a swift *Yes.*

Next, it's Brad's turn.

"Do you know of a journal or diary that may be hidden somewhere in the house?"

No.

Rob asks Pauly whether she is the person who has been heard to say "hello" in the house. Although the answer is no, Pauly claims that they do indeed know the lady in question — but cannot tell us her name.

Rob's wondering whether Pauly has a favorite room or part of the house. When the planchette indicates that she does, Rob asks them to spell it out. The answer — *Top* — seems to imply the third floor, but the board corrects us; what *Top* in fact means, is the Widow's Walk. Apparently Pauly enjoys standing up there and watching the world go by for miles around...and who can blame her?

"The Widow's Walk has the best view in the entire house," Heather observes, speaking softly. The planchette shoots directly to *Yes,* in complete agreement. The participants break up with laughter, keeping their fingers on the planchette, but clearly tickled by the fact that Pauly has weighed in without being specifically asked. It's starting to feel more like an actual conversation than some Victorian-esque parlor trick.

This is confirmed when I ask Pauly whether she's enjoying the camaraderie as much as we are. The answer is a very enthusiastic yes.

Now it's time for Heather to pose the question which has been on her mind since the very beginning. "Pauly...are you the person who sits on Noa's bed, and watches over her while she sleeps?"

We all watch the planchette like hawks.

The answer is not the one we expect. It is spelled out slowly and with apparent reluctance.

S-O-R-R-Y.

"Oh, no!" Heather is mortified at having her question taken the wrong way. "Don't be sorry. It's a *lovely* thing for you to be doing, Pauly."

There's a definite maternal vibe to this. Noa has never felt frightened or creeped out by the presence of an unseen watcher in her room. The door apparently locking itself was a different story, but we're not going to jump in and assume that Pauly was responsible for doing that.

"I love it," Noa smiles. "I really do. I find it very comforting, Pauly...and I just want to say thank you."

Tears are welling up in my eyes. Looking around the Speakeasy, I can see that I'm not the only one. The idea that a protective female spirit, one who probably misses her own children, is keeping a watchful eye on young Noa, is making us all feel rather emotional. It's moments such as this which one tends to remember as the years pass, standing out from the countless hours spent in haunted houses where absolutely nothing is happening. It feels as though we have made a connection here; a connection which has its own unique kind of ineffable beauty.

Love You, spells out the board.

"Now I'm *really* having a moment," I mumble. Nobody is making eye contact with one another, because we all have happy tears running down our cheeks...except for Brad, who likes to pretend he has a heart of ice.

Heather has another question for the watchful spirit. "Pauly, do you ever happen to see a black dog in Noa's room?"

Yes, she does.

Noa's ecstatic to hear this. This is her dog, Fire, who passed a while back.

"Thank you," Heather begins, but Pauly isn't finished. She goes on to spell out the word *Cat.*

Stephen hasn't revealed anything up to this point, but a fellow medium (who is completely unaware of Stephen's location) has just told him that this place has the spirit of a strong male who dresses primarily in black, two girls...and a cat.

Noa is grinning at the thought that she has not just the spirit of a woman watching over her, but also a phantom dog and a cat hanging out up there. All the fun of having animal friends, but she doesn't have to feed them.

I ask Pauly whether Satan, Pork and Beans ever see that dog. A strong *Yes.* "Do they have doggy play dates?" Again, a very strong yes. We all laugh. Now we have an idea exactly what it is that is setting them off, when the Blumbergs themselves can see nothing.

"Pauly, do you ever encounter an older English gentleman walking around on the third floor?" Heather asks, changing the subject slightly.

"I feel attacked," I mumble, earning myself some side eye from the family matriarch.

Pauly says that she does.

"Is he also watching over Noa?"

A strong *Yes.*

"I'm sure that's my grandfather," Heather murmurs.

The planchette slowly, deliberately spells out the words *Grand Yes.*

Nobody looks at Heather. She is obviously deeply moved. The happy tears just got a little happier.

After a moment, I ask Pauly whether she would like it if, in future, Heather and Noa were to come down to the Speakeasy with a talking board of their own and have chats with her. The answer is a very enthusiastic yes. I'm all too aware that tomorrow is our last day in Dresden, and I don't want to see Pauly left without any company or interaction, now that we've opened this particular door to communicating with her.

Noa and Heather love the idea.

The planchette begins moving again. This time, its motion is slower; it's still very deliberate, but the speed of movement has been cut in half. It quickly becomes clear why.

Tired is spelled out.

We're reading this message loud and clear, but just to be sure, I ask whether Pauly would like to have a little rest. The planchette dithers for a moment, then creeps across the board again, first to YES, and then to goodbye.

Everybody present says goodbye to Pauly and wishes her the very best. Stephen closes down the board, emphasizing that no negativity or darkness is permitted to linger or attach itself to anybody in the room. The door which we opened has just been shut, firmly, securely, but with the intent that Heather and Noa will be able to open it again in future whenever they so choose.

This is our opportunity to give Noa a little education on the use of talking boards — more specifically, how to safely open one with clear boundaries, and to close it down appropriately at the end of the session. Just like the days of Yahoo chat rooms, which were gone before Noa was born, you only have the word of whoever's coming through the talking board that they really are who they say they are. *Trust, but verify,* is the message we're hoping to instill. I've a feeling that Noa will be a diligent student when it comes to this stuff.

That was a particularly moving session, everybody agrees. Even Brad had the slightest glimmer of emotion when Pauly was telling her story.

"A mere eye twitch," Heather grins at him.

"That was dust," Brad counters, making us all laugh.

Before we file upstairs, there's just one last order of business. It's not a pleasant thing, but I have to make sure of it because I know that the skeptics who will ultimately read this book will think of it right away.

Let's say for a moment that the Blumbergs are grifters (which they aren't) and that they're trying to stage a haunting for their own benefit; for the fame, for some perceived financial gain, or whatever. It's something I've seen unscrupulous location owners do in the past. If that were the case, then it would be child's play for Arryn to text Heather the number he wrote on the piece of paper, at the beginning of our Ouija session. Heather could take a quick look, and without any of us suspecting, nudge the planchette in the direction of those two specific numbers — *et voila*, we're all impressed, and we give credit to the ghosts.

I'm blushing before I even ask the question, but there's no avoiding it.

"Heather, may I please see your phone?"

Without hesitation, she unlocks it and hands it over.

"May I please see your last texts from Arryn?"

She doesn't ask why. She just opens up the text chain and lets me read every message that has been exchanged between herself and her husband in the past 24 hours. None of them mentions Ouija boards. There are no numbers at all — specifically no 87 or 78. Nothing.

There *is* a strange photograph of audiobook narrator Josh Heard, wearing only a Stars and Stripes-themed bikini, posing against the handlebars of a Harley Davidson. He's holding a sign which reads "I brake for Johnny Houser."

(Alright, this part didn't actually happen. It's one of only two outright lies you'll encounter in this book. The other is coming up shortly, when Arryn says: "I've made you a drink and there's hardly any alcohol in it." Apparently, the word "hardly" has a radically different meaning in South Africa).

Shamefaced, I explain to Heather why I needed to see her phone. Not that I had any reason to doubt the Blumbergs' integrity before, but now I can shoot down the notion that they may have conspired in order to transmit that specific number to the Ouija board.

To her credit, and my eternal gratitude, Heather accepts my rationale and doesn't appear to hold it against me. In the aftermath of the Ouija session, our collective mood might best be described as happy/sad. We file upstairs one at a time. Toad is wandering around the living room, quite happily snuffling at any floor pucky he can find and enjoying the buffet of new sights, sounds, and smells. This house has got to be an absolute playground for him, just as it has been for us.

John and Jessica are hanging out with Arryn. They have just spent some time investigating the laundry room, a part of the house we haven't hit yet, and Heather and Arryn's bedroom and ensuite bathroom.

I've never heard Jessica claim to be psychic, sensitive, or anything of that nature, but she tells me after the tour that the only place she sensed anything out of the ordinary was in the Blumbergs' master bathroom on the second floor. That's particularly interesting, in light of the EVP we got in there before their arrival.

"We heard some weird, loud knocks," Jessica says.

"Sounded like somebody tapping directly on the microphone," Tenney explains. "We heard them in the room as well, but playing them back on the tape, it sounded like direct contact with the mic itself."

So, the Weirdos heard a mix of loud knocks on the walls, and even louder knocks on the recording during playback. For comparison, Jessica tapped her nails on the walls, and determined that the knocks were equally loud.

"It was almost as if something was testing out the microphone," Tenney muses. Jessica nods in agreement.

These guys are experienced investigators. They're well accustomed to the ordinary sounds that a house makes when it's settling, or just simply going about the business of being a house. If they say that these noises were not that, then I believe them.

Tenney adds that the taps didn't actually start until Jessica requested them. Once they moved up to the master bathroom, they heard what sounded like a group of men in conversation. This was definitely not the sound from our rather hushed Ouija session in the Speakeasy carrying upstairs. Jessica and John are savvy enough to know the difference, and it began before we had even started our Ouija session. We know this for sure because Tim was helping coordinate things.

"It sounded like a group having a meeting," Jessica adds. This is very similar to what Heather has experienced herself in the house; something which neither Jessica nor John was aware of. "It sounded very serious, not fun."

"Very businesslike," agrees Tenney. He points out that, given the property's stature in the community, it's almost certain that a number of high money conversations happened in here over the years. "What happened downstairs that has everybody so teary-eyed?"

I give them a run-down on the Pauly situation, so we're all on the same page.

Over in the Chapel, Arryn is mixing up a drink for anybody who wants them — designated drivers excepted. After a long and productive day of investigating, it's time for us all to hang out and be social. Tenney launches into a long string of truly appalling Dad jokes. "Oh God," Jessica rolls her eyes, "don't start with that elephant shit."

But it's too late. We don't know at the time what "that elephant shit" is, but we're about to find out, because Tenney launches into an all-out assault of elephant gags that ought to get him sentenced to five to ten years in the punitentiary.

Jessica's right.

They're bad.

"Jesus Christ," she groans as he fires off the first of many. "No-one's gonna laugh."

A sample:

"How do you know if an elephant's in your refrigerator?

"—There's footprints in the butter."

Oh dear.

"How many elephants can you fit in a Volkswagen Bug?" We shake our heads, clueless. "Four. Two in the back, two in the front."

Um.

"How can you tell if there's four elephants in your refrigerator?

"—There's a Volkswagen Bug parked out front."

I can feel my status as the self-proclaimed king of dad jokes plummeting right in front of my eyes.

"What's white and sits in a tree?

"— A refrigerator."

"THAT ONE IS *NOT* A JOKE," Jessica insists.

"Why shouldn't you go in the jungle between 4 and 5 in the afternoon?

"—That's when the refrigerators fall out of the trees."

"THAT'S. **NOT. A**. JOKE!"

"Do you know why pygmies are so small?"

"—Because they go into the jungle between 4 and 5 in the afternoon..."

We're laughing. We can't help ourselves. Heather has tears streaming down her face again, but this time, they're tears of laughter. "He. Just. Won't. Stop!" she sobs in between breaths.

And she's right. He won't. The elephant jokes just keep coming, punctuated by laughter and regular "That's not a joke!" comments from Jessica, who has presumably heard all of these elephant-related nightmares countless times before. Bless her, the poor woman looks as though her best friend has just pissed in her Wheaties...again.

"Make mine a double," Brad deadpans from the bar. Arryn sympathetically upends the bottle and makes it a triple pineapple vodka.

Who could blame him?

We hang out and chat, enjoying good company and Arryn's talents as a purveyor of liquid treats. (Say it with me again, friends — drink responsibly).

Foremost on the mind of everybody who attended the Speakeasy Ouija session is Pauly. I catch myself making furtive glances around the room, looking past the small clusters of friends chatting to one another, and wondering whether she's also hanging out with us, enjoying the happy vibes that are going on.

Toad meanders by. I snag him and scritch behind his ears. For all we know, the living room and Chapel could be *filled* with dead people, drawn to the positive energy that's being generated in here. The atmosphere in the house right now is absolutely joyful, and I've always believed that spirits can feed upon that sort of positivity just as they can on darker, more negative emotions.

The only sad note is that it's Brad and Tim's last night with us. Tomorrow morning, the two Yoopers have to hit the road and make the return trip to Michigan. It's been a pleasure having them along on the first of what will turn out to be many adventures in the paranormal field.

We spend the next few hours just chatting, listening to Tenney tell stories (of which he has about a million, many of which are legendary) and share insights. Sometimes, this approach yields dividends in terms of voice phenomena. Alas, that is not to be the case today either.

That's okay. The spirits of the funeral home have spoken aplenty. They aren't performing tricks for our amusement or edification. It's entirely up to them exactly how much or how little they're going to interact with us, or anybody else. The level of engagement we've had from them thus far has been immensely gratifying. Every single member of my team appreciates it.

"Here, try this," the bearded bartender places a drink into my hand that looks as though it ought to be fizzing, like the beaker in some mad scientist's lab. There's hardly any alcohol in it."

Bullshit.

By the time the drink is gone, my legs are drunk. It's time for me to switch to Diet Coke. With hindsight, it's definitely wise for me to stop at one drink, after learning beyond a shadow of a doubt that Arryn and I have vastly different definitions of the phrase "hardly any alcohol."

Tenney and Arryn get into an involved discussion about the finer points of their shared interest, *Star Trek*. Heather and Jessica are deep in conversation about an array of topics. The rest of us simply hang out and unwind after the breakneck pace of the past three days.

It's getting late, and after a round of hugs is exchanged, we all head back to our respective accommodations for the night. Tonight, it's a little bit more challenging for me to fall asleep. My mind keeps drifting back to Pauly and hoping that she doesn't feel too sad about her current situation. I'm cheered up by the knowledge that she couldn't wish for a better adoptive family than the Blumbergs to share a home with. Hopefully tomorrow, that home will share some more of its secrets with us.

On that note, I fall into a deep and dreamless sleep.

Chapter Twenty-Two

Arryn's Adult Beverages - Bitter Pill

B itter Pill

    1. 1.5 oz Beefeater Gin (or any other reasonably priced London dry gin, just don't use any of the ones that are flavored)

    2. 0.25 oz Martini & Rossi Bitter 1872

    3. 0.25 oz Lillet Blanc

    4. 2-3 drops Peychaud's Bitters

    5. 2 oz Grapefruit juice (fresh squeezed is the best, but I often use Tropicana...also, as long as it's not sweetened or a cocktail you should be fine)

    6. Add all the ingredients to a large shaker full of ice

    7. Shake well then taste, you want something that is bitter as a top note followed by a little sweetness and herbaceousness, think Negroni or Aperol spritz with less sugar

8.   Pour into any good wine glass about ¼ full of ice (I use squat mid-century modern vintage wine glasses Heather got at an estate sale for me)

9.   Don't fill all the way! Leave a good inch to half an inch at the top of the glass

10.   Top with Veuve Clicquot Brut Champagne (the champagne will add the sweetness and effervesce to counteract the almost too bitter cocktail base)

11.   Drink with satisfaction as you would any great *aperitivo*

Chapter Twenty-Three

Mysteries Uncovered

Friday is our fourth and final day in Dresden. It begins with our now traditional breakfast get-together, after which we say a sad goodbye to Brad and Tim. There are hugs and farewells. Everybody is convinced that we'll all do this together again sometime in the future, whether it's a return visit to the house, or some other weird and wonderful location.

"So much has happened over the last few days," Tim reflects between sips of coffee. "I'm still trying to process it all."

"The activity level that we've been capturing in the house is something we seldom get," Brad chimes in. "Every night we left, I felt physically drained."

"Same here," his partner in crime agrees. "I've rarely slept so well."

"Physically *and* mentally drained," Brad goes on, between bites of food. "There has been no malevolence at all, despite the fact that some of the messages have been quite dark."

"It feels so comforting in there, I think mainly because of the family's positive energy."

"The family is such a lively force, they're such wonderful and strong people, that I wouldn't worry about the potential for any type of oppression." Brad shifts in his chair slightly. "It's such a warm and comforting atmosphere."

Tim notes that the Estes sessions we've held at the funeral home are unlike any others he has ever seen. "If you saw this on reality TV, you'd never believe it. This house has a definite personality."

Our conversation turns to the Blumbergs. Brad observes that the family has done nothing to make him question their sincerity or integrity. We all agree that their dynamic and colorful personalities are probably a factor in the haunting. There's a lot of potential energy there to be tapped, if you're a spirit who's on the hunt for a free "meal."

We wish the lads safe travels on their six hour-long drive, then get into our own car and hit the road for Dresden.

Once again, slobber-chops Satan and his two doggy compadres meet us at the door. Arryn tells us that once again, the family did not enjoy an uninterrupted night's sleep. At precisely 2:22 in the morning, they were woken by a howl coming from within the house. Pork, Beans and Satan were accounted for. None of them were the source of the sound, which was ear-splittingly loud.

"The dogs do occasionally have bad dreams, and they'll wake up howling," Arryn tells us. "We know what that sounds like. This was not that. It was more of a guttural shout. It came from the area of the Pink Room, or the bottom of the stairs."

I immediately think of the Lady in Blue. Could this be a replay of the sound she made when she fell to her death — or is something equally peculiar but different actually going on here?

The big, bad beastie named Pork was so freaked out that he came into the master bedroom and slept at the foot of Heather and Arryn's bed. He usually decamps to the more comfortable couch, but not this time. Pork wasn't letting his parents out of his sight.

"There was a mournful, grieving side to this howl," Heather recalls. "I felt quite nervous afterward, after waking up in a cold sweat. The howl went on for a while. Arryn and I debated what it was, but we never went to check it out."

Once the nerve-wracking howl stopped, there followed two very loud, solid bangs, as though something very heavy had fallen over.

It doesn't escape our attention that two nights ago, something very similar happened. Arryn and Heather were woken up "at about 2:20am" by a loud cry within the house. There were no bangs that time, but the frightening audible phenomenon sounds very similar, and the timing is so close, I won't buy that it's a coincidence. After searching the house that time, nothing was out of place. The same was true when they got up earlier this morning. Of whatever had caused the two loud bangs, there was absolutely no sign. Nothing had fallen. Nothing was missing. There were no signs of intrusion. Once again, the other members of the household slept right through the disturbance.

The team is anxious to begin investigating, but first, I'm bringing in my friend, psychic medium MJ Dickson. As previously mentioned, she lives in the UK and is going to do her best to remote view the house to see what she can pick up. Thanks to the wonders of modern technology — Skype — we're able to speak clearly with one another. Today she's on holiday in New Orleans.

Usually, MJ works blind; I go to great lengths to keep her in the dark as to the nature and identity of the location. That hasn't been possible this time out, because we've all been social media whores this week, and keeping a lid on the news just wasn't feasible. So, playing Devil's Advocate, anything that was aired on the TV show or is out there on the Internet, is something she could conceivably already know by conventional means.

We begin our walkthrough reading in the Speakeasy. MJ has taken some notes in advance and tells me that she's picking up on a woman with two girls, each of whom has an S-name. I jot that down for future reference.

Although she can't identify which object is specifically the cause, MJ tells us that paranormal activity has recently picked up in the vicinity of the parlor because of an item or artifact that has come into the house very recently. I mute the mic so that MJ can't hear us. Heather reveals that she has brought in several different things over the past couple of weeks, ranging from furniture to books to a skull, of all things, and confirms that yes, the atmosphere in that room has completely changed since then.

Next, MJ tells us that she's seeing animals acting or reacting strangely, growling and staring at nothing, in the vicinity of a staircase. That tracks, but it's also something we saw on the TV show, so I throw that out as potential evidence and we move on.

She's also seeing a woman in a Victorian-era prairie dress, with dark hair tied back in a bun. What's interesting about that is that during our Ouija board sessions, Heather had a brief mental flash of a female who looked *exactly* like that. It's an interesting synchronicity, and I'm wondering if this could be the woman who has been shushing Heather and Brad during their Estes sessions.

MJ is suddenly giggling up a storm. I ask her about the cause, and in between laughs, she reveals that she has just heard one of the spirits refer to Brad as "the gassy one." Now we're cracking up too. I make a mental note to start referring to him as Count Flatula from now on.

Now that she's tuning into the house, I'm surprised to hear that she isn't picking up much in the Cigar Lounge. We step out into the Speakeasy. My camera is switched off, so she's not able to pick up any visual cues. MJ has no idea what part of the house we're in.

"I'm picking up on music playing, and it's getting louder," she tells us as I walk closer to the record player and the long rows of vinyl albums which line one wall. That's an impressive synchronicity, considering that this is also the part of the house where Heather has heard music in the past.

She isn't picking up on much else down here. We move out into the basement hallway. "There's a young girl — around ten, maybe eleven years old. Man...I'm getting so many flashes, all these images...it's very chaotic and hard to read clearly."

This is the first time I've heard of MJ having such a reaction to a haunted location.

"I'm assuming this is a bedroom," she goes on, as we step into Doc's bedroom, then keep moving through the basement level then climb to the ground floor. She psychically picks up on a thin-faced, mustachioed man wearing a bowler hat. "I feel as though he whistles in this area a lot, and that his footsteps are heard here a lot."

Disembodied footsteps are indeed heard in this part of the house. Even more interesting, MJ is convinced that he would sometimes put his hands on the shoulders of the living. I'm instantly reminded of Heather feeling hands on her shoulders during our Estes session two days ago. Equally fascinating is the fact that one of the AI-generated images displayed — you guessed it — a man wearing a bowler hat and sporting a mustache.

Wandering into the dining room, an abashed MJ tells us that for some reason, she's getting a strong psychic impression of...parrots.

Heather looks like she's about to choke.

Directly underneath the dining table, there are two carved wooden parrots.

Wow.

The sheer specificity of this hit is impressive, and I can't explain it away conventionally.

"Well, we'll always have parrots..." I really can't help myself sometimes. Nobody dignifies the awful pun with a response.

"Bowler hat man is following you around," MJ announces as Heather leads us down the steps to her store. We descend a level, and she feels as though there has been a structural change, as though we've passed through a wall that we "weren't supposed to."

That's right on the money. The part of the funeral home that houses her shop is not original. It is an extension, added on to the main building later. It was used as a garage for the hearses.

"Are you near any coffins or caskets?" our psychic friend asks. "I'm hearing a voice repeating the word *coffin* over and over again — but of course, you are in a funeral home, so..."

Heather jabs a finger at the wall behind me. On the other side, not three feet away from where I'm standing, is the casket-turned-bar which adorns the Speakeasy.

Our next stop is the master bedroom and bathroom on the second floor. MJ tells me that we're very near the spot where the lady in the dress is active. At first, I'm wondering whether this could be Pauly, but then MJ gives her an age of late twenties or early thirties. Pauly was older than that when she died, although there is the school of thought which says that spirits can choose to manifest as they appeared in the prime of their life, or at whatever age they wish.

It's possible that she's picking up on the Lady in Blue, though I remind myself that MJ didn't pick up anything as we climbed the staircase past the point at which her apparition is traditionally seen. Only later, when I learn about the female EVP that we recorded in the master bathroom, will I connect that phenomenon with what MJ is telling us right now. Could she be the woman who angrily hissed *"STOP!"* at us?

This is also the part of the house in which, we're told, a female once died.

"This is a spirit that likes reaching out to the living, physically. I think that wherever you are right now, people sometimes feel a hand brushing across their back, shoulder or arm…"

"Happens all the time," Heather mouths at me. Whether this touch comes from the mysterious woman, or from the man with the mustache, is unclear. Another mystery for us to get to the bottom of.

Climbing the stairs again, we make our way into Noa's bedroom. The camera is still off.

"I'm seeing paintings, bright, vibrant colors," MJ says, which is a pretty accurate description of the murals which adorn her bedroom walls. She's also seeing a painting of a woman, which is not a hit, from what I can see.

MJ is apologetic that she can't get anything more, yet as far as we're concerned, she's given us plenty to think about already. There were several hits — the parrots, the music, the coffin, the man with the mustache — which in my view, can't be attributed to mere guesswork.

I enjoy working with her, and in my opinion, her remote viewing capabilities have been developing with each different session she views.

She's going from strength to strength, and I'm excited to put her to the test again during future projects.

Right now, it's time for MJ to sign off. The delights and temptations of New Orleans are calling, and she doesn't want to be late. Thanking her for her time and efforts, I end the audio recording session and hang up Skype.

I give voice to what we're all thinking:

"Let's go get some caffeine."

Vickie Trickett is a tattoo artist and a friend of Heather's. She's responsible for the new tattoos that Jill and Stephen are now sporting, after visiting her studio to get themselves a permanent memento of this expedition.

She's a regular visitor to the house, and has come over to see us, at Heather's request. It promises to be an interesting interview. After we settle into chairs in the Speakeasy, facing one another, I ask a few basic warm-up questions before we get to the meat of the matter.

"I don't tell a lot of people," she says hesitantly, before telling me that she is a sensitive, capable of sensing and sometimes seeing spirits. I always try to keep an open mind whenever somebody tells me this, being as non-judgmental as possible. It's usually not something that can definitively be proved or disproved. "It really isn't anybody's business but mine."

She's right about that. Although Vickie consents to me including this in the book, it sits better with me that she doesn't seek any kind of publicity for it. I've seen people making the same claim and showboating, trying to become the center of attention (when the spotlight really belongs to the spirits). Vickie isn't that way, and I find her complete lack of desire for fame or recognition to be convincing.

"I just pick up on certain things," she elaborates, "and while I don't really understand it, I've learned to accept it."

This raises the question: what must it have been like for a sensitive to walk into a house like this — was it the paranormal equivalent of Disney's *Haunted Mansion?*

"It was a little overwhelming," she admits. "There was a lot going on. It sounded as though thirty people were whispering all at once, but none of it was clear enough to make out the words."

She singles out the Speakeasy as being one of the chattier parts of the house, which tracks with Heather's experiences. This part of the house feels very claustrophobic and staticky to Vickie, a "dirty, icky" sensation that leaves her feeling unclean.

Something rather disturbing happened to her when she was in the house working on a photoshoot. Vickie was in the second-floor room in which the hanging was said to have taken place. From out of nowhere, she felt herself slammed up against the wall by an unseen force. Vickie was held there for the span of five seconds, during which time she was completely unable to breathe. Her neck felt constricted.

Almost no sooner than it happened, she was released. At the time of Vickie's deeply disturbing encounter, she had no idea about the death which local rumor claim had happened in there. Learning of it only made the incident seem even more chilling than before.

It is not a room she no longer cares to visit.

Equally busy, in a paranormal sense, is Noa's floor, the third.

"There's a gentleman and a young boy up there," she tells me. "The boy was younger, and I can't tell whether it's a father and son, or a younger brother and an older brother."

This immediately brings to mind the playful young boy that put in an appearance during Jill and Kat's mirror scrying session. Playing hide-and-go-seek on the staircase.

"There are also two little girls on that floor," Vickie goes on, "and also an adult lady. I don't know how everybody is related to one another."

The little girls, which she says are around seven and eight years old and may be sisters, are always together. Their relationship to the woman is unclear. She might be their mother, a governess, or something else. But if the stories we've heard from multiple sources are correct, it's clear that the third floor has no shortage of ghostly inhabitants to keep Noa company.

Just as we're speculating about the possible connections between this gaggle of spirits, Vickie suddenly trails off, her gaze shifting to focus on something over my shoulder.

"What?" I ask.

"Um."

"*What?*" I turn around. There's nothing behind me. Just the colorful glow of the casket bar.

"The young boy just walked past you," she laughs, shaking her head. This is an everyday occurrence for her. I feel a chill run down my spine. Vickie is unfazed. "Now he's gone."

Vickie believes that he is attracted to Noa — not in a romantic way, but simply because she is the closest thing to somebody his own age. He's seeking friendship the only way he knows how.

He has disappeared through the door into the garage...a door that remains closed.

Vickie favors me with a wry smile. I, on the other hand, haven't seen a thing. Nor did I feel a cold draft, or any other kind of physical manifestation that might indicate the proximity of a ghostly child.

As the old saying goes: *Always a bridesmaid, never a bride.*

We're down Jim, Brad, and Tim. The Terrible Trio of Weirdos is having a local adventure and will be joining us later this afternoon.

That leaves Stephen, Jill, Rob, Heather and I to our own devices for a while. Over tea and coffee, we decide to give the room in which a former resident hanged themselves another try.

As the Estes Method wasn't particularly effective here last time, we opt for a talking board instead. It's obviously a very delicate situation, one that calls for tact, respect, and above all, compassion. Additionally, it would be making a leap to assume that whoever we may end up communicating with in this room is necessarily the person who lost their life here. It's not as if the house isn't teeming with potential communicators, based on what we've experienced so far.

Stephen opens the board, charging it with positive energy and setting the expectation that only honest, truthful communication will be permitted. Jill opens by asking for the communicator's name. The planchette spells out *RUNICE*...which looks like gibberish at first. It's Stephen who cottons on to the fact that it spells out a form of *"Are you nice?"*

We assure the board that we are indeed nice. *NOA HEPE* is given as the communicator's name. Although it's tempting to assume that this pertains to Noa, the rest of the message doesn't mean much that we can discern.

"How old are you?" Jill asks. The planchette bobs across to the 1 and then the 4.

Fourteen.

This gets me thinking. The odds of a 14-year-old child spirit named either Noa or Noah being present in the house seem pretty steep. It's not exactly a common name. There's a hypothesis out there that some talking board communications can be coming, not from the spirits of the dead or discarnate intelligences located elsewhere in space, time, or some other dimension — but rather, that they may originate in the subconscious minds of the living. This is why I made a point of not letting anybody other than Arryn know which two-digit number he was going to write and place on the kitchen countertop. It's conceivable that the Ouija board was trying to read the number telepathically from Arryn's subconscious mind.

By the same token, could it be that we're now conversing with some subset of Noa Blumberg's mind — a part that thinks it's fourteen years old?

Stranger things have happened.

However, that gets blown out of the water when Heather asks whether we're speaking with a boy. The board immediately responds with *Yes*.

So much for that theory.

We ask for the name again, and we're given the name *"Clark."* He denies having ever lived in the house. I-D-I-E comes next.

"You died in this house?" Heather asks sadly. Yes, and his funeral was also held here. Noah tells us that he's here because he likes it here, which is heartwarming. I suspect that the family atmosphere cultivated by the Blumbergs might play a big role in that, as could the presence of a young person close to his own age — Noa.

"Could you leave if you wanted to?" I'm curious.

Yes.

This young chap tells us that he isn't compelled to stay in the house all the time. He has the freedom to roam, though exactly how far is not something he's able to tell us. Jill asks where he was born, and we're given the answer *Chatham,* the nearest town.

Heather asks whether Clark is a Mennonite, a reasonable guess considering that there's a sizable Mennonite population living in the vicinity. He tells us that he died 109 years ago; that he helped on his parents' farm; and that he didn't enjoy it, wishing that he'd been able to go to school and get an education instead.

Clark admits that he likes playing with the dogs sometimes, perhaps explaining why Pork, Beans and Satan will react to apparently thin air. He'd like to talk to Noa, but hasn't tried to make himself heard so far because he's...

The planchette spells out the word *afraid*. This clearly saddens Heather, as it would doubtless sadden Noa too. "Noa would be very open to talking to you," Heather says.

"Is it because she's a young lady?" I ask.

"She's not *that* much of a lady," her mother says archly. She asks whether Clark is aware of the male entity she has seen walking around the house. Apparently, he hasn't, implying that these two particular entities exist in different silos, as it were. We've encountered layered hauntings in the past; cases in which spirits from different eras co-exist in the same place, but are unaware of one another, despite occupying the same physical space.

Stephen asks whether Clark heard the loud cries in the wee small hours of the morning earlier this week. He did, and while he can't (or won't) tell us the identity of whoever was responsible for them, Clark does say that they are not friendly. Heather takes this in her stride. Their intent was to scare the Blumbergs for fun, the board reveals.

Getting down to brass tacks, we ask how many children are in the house along with him. *Eight boys and ten girls* is the answer. That raises eyebrows around the room. None of us expected the number to be quite that high. Interestingly, Clark does not know of any spirit in this room which relates to the tragedy that's said to have taken place here. He does tell us, however, that Raff and Doc are watched over by "lots" of spirits. I wonder what the rational, logical young fellows will make of that.

It's been a pleasant session, but the energy in the planchette is beginning to wane. This suggests that things are starting to wind down. Stephen closes down the board, letting Clark know that there will be other opportunities to communicate at a later time.

Jill is keen to give her scrying mirror a try. Scrying is an age-old method of attempting to communicate with the spirit world, other realms, or to divine information by paranormal means. It involves gazing into a reflective surface, most often a mirror (though water is also a popular medium), for prolonged periods, in the hope of entering a higher state of consciousness.

Low light conditions are optimal for scrying. The dim red glow in the Speakeasy is ideally suited for it. Jill sets up her mirror carefully on the tabletop and adjusts her chair, placing herself squarely in front of it.

Just to make things more interesting, I've arranged for a friend and fellow investigator to do the same thing at a remote location. My good friend Kat Armstrong has set up her own scrying mirror at her home in Iowa. My hope is that by coordinating both scrying sessions to begin and end at the same time and using an open phone line to link the two, we might see some interesting results.

I set up a video call to Kat's number. Her face pops up on my screen. After we exchange pleasantries, I shut off the camera and microphone, so that Kat can't hear us (we can hear her) and therefore we won't contaminate her results. She's sitting in front of her own mirror, working by candlelight.

For the first few minutes, all we have is silence. Both Jill and Kat are "tuning in" in their own respective ways, which tend to be unique to the individual, and very personal.

Five minutes later, Kat begins to perceive the figure of a woman taking form in front of her eyes. She has shoulder-length, straight brown hair, with a pair of bangs framing her forehead.

"She's beckoning or waving, as though somebody is supposed to follow her," Kat says, "but it doesn't look as though anybody is around. It isn't her that's important for you to know about. She's trying to show us somebody else...somebody that you're missing."

I unmute. "Please let me know if you can zero in on whoever that somebody else is," I ask, before muting the mic again.

That somebody turns out to be a man, although Kat is having a hard time discerning further details. As time passes, she gets the impression that he died of a medical ailment relating to the left side of his abdomen. It was a painful death. I'm not sure what message he's trying to get across..."

Now, Jill is also picking up on a male. However, she's getting blocked by something positioned off to her right. Whatever it is, it's deliberately distracting her, Jill says, her brow creased in concentration. This feels like a deliberate attempt to distract her. Then something touches the back of her neck. We can clearly see that nobody physical is behind her; our team members are all sitting in chairs positioned around the periphery of the room.

Once again, we're being deliberately thwarted when we try to close in on the truth.

"It's a different way of saying shush," Rob observes.

"Exactly," Jill nods. "Whatever it is that's being hidden, it's something big..."

She goes back to scrying, trying to break through the interference.

Both Jill and Kat start to see a white, human-shaped figure in their peripheral vision. It's notable that Kat cannot hear Jill describing what she sees, so there's no way she could be influenced by it. (The reverse is not true, I should point out in the interest of balance).

Finally, her frustration apparent, Jill gives up. Not wanting to call it quits just yet, we put Rob in her place, to see whether switching out the observer will yield different results.

Kat senses that the spirits of the house really appreciate what the Blumbergs are doing to restore and maintain it now. That's got to come as welcome news to Heather and her family, who have put so much sweat equity (not to mention *actual* financial equity) into the place.

Suddenly, Kat's seeing a male entity staring back at her. His face is distorting and twisting, though whether this is being done deliberately or not remains open to question. The man appears to be in a space where there are tree branches framing his head. This can only be one place in the house: the main entrance hallway which has been decorated with an enchanted forest-type theme.

"He's showing himself with melting skin," Kat says, the distaste evident in her voice, "so I'm going to let him go away."

She does, performing the psychic equivalent of disconnecting by hanging up the phone...at least, she *tries* to. He really doesn't want to go away, Kat notes, adding that he seems to find the concept of scrying intriguing. It's making him understandably curious.

Then, his face stabilizes. He's a thinly built man with a stubbly chin, and fair hair.

Now a few minutes into his own scrying session, Rob is seeing nothing but the color blue. From off to my left, behind the glass doors of the Cigar Lounge, comes the sound of movement. I turn to look. Nothing is moving. Nothing is out of place. The sound stops.

Whatever that was, it was more than the building settling...but I don't know *what* it was.

"I didn't mention it earlier," Rob says, "but I was down here earlier, on my own, taking some video footage for TikTok. That door opened up all by itself."

Still peering into the scrying mirror, he nods his head in the direction of the door which leads through to Heather's shop. I recall checking the door earlier on and finding that it closes pretty solidly. It's not the kind of door that would simply pop open without some sort of stimulus.

Kat picks up on the presence of a ginger-haired little boy, aged somewhere between six and eight years old, who she says likes to play on the stairs. The staircase in question is clearly the master, because she's scrying the stairs curving up and around a corner, with the little boy poking his head over the banister at the very top. It feels like a game of hide and go seek, with the young boy impatiently waiting for somebody to come after him.

"He's wearing a little green sweater, with a button-up collared shirt underneath, and brown trousers," Kat says. I make a note. This may be valuable information for future investigators of the house. We're all relieved to hear that his vibe is a very happy one, playful and joyous. Whether he's an intelligent entity or a residual phenomenon, I'm not entirely sure. From the way in which she's describing him, I'm guessing it's the former, not the latter.

Next comes a male voice, speaking to Kat and passing on a message for the Blumbergs. Whether or not this comes from the face-changing man is unclear. The message this unidentified male wants to convey to Heather, Arryn, Noa and Raff is that the more paranormal investigation takes place in the house, the more the spirits will be drawn to it. While not necessarily threatening, it is certainly something that the family needs to take on board before embarking on Ouija board and Estes Method sessions here.

There's a reason so many paranormal investigators refuse to investigate their own homes, after all...

Both Kat and Rob are now seeing a white square in their respective mirrors. I'm intrigued by this, as Kat can't know that Rob is seeing it. Jill feels something lightly brush again her right cheek, almost a caress. Then it happens again. She isn't remotely intimidated by it. This is par for the course for Jill.

I check the time. Thirty minutes have passed. It's time for us to shut down the link and move on to trying something else. Thanking Kat for her time, we disconnect, ending both of our scrying sessions. The mirrors are to be shut down, just as one should down a talking board. In our view, it's rarely a good idea to leave ajar a door that one has opened up. You never know quite who — or what — is going to come through it.

Chapter Twenty-Four

Arryn's Adult Beverages - Staycation

S *taycation*

   1. *1 oz Malibu Coconut Rum*

2. *1 oz Appleton Estate Signature Rum*

3. *0.5 oz Alize Gold Passion Liqueur (this makes all the difference to this cocktail, it gives an acidic passion fruit kick that is hard to replicate, this liqueur is great in so many drinks or just add a shot to a glass of great champagne)*

4. *Bar spoon Aperol*

5. *3-4 drops Peychaud's Bitters*

6. *0.75 oz fresh squeezed lime juice*

7.   *0.75 oz Mosambi - Sweet Lime - Dabur Real Fruit Power (best to look in your local Indian speciality store or Amazon)*

8.   *Add everything to a heavy shaker full of ice and shake like you're in a rush to get back in the pool*

9.   *Serve over ice in a chilled tumbler*

10.   *Drink slowly thinking of that time you had too much rum punch while out snorkeling in the Caribbean (which Heather and I have done many times when we lived in Barbados - Rodey we miss you!)*

Chapter Twenty-Five

Wrapping Up

John, Jessica and Toad have spent the day exploring the delights of Dresden and its surrounding area. This includes visiting historic sites related to the Underground Railroad and abolition; then they ransack thrift shops and used bookstores, picking up some "killer bargains" along the way. Now they're here and ready to rock.

It's time to investigate.

Most of our equipment arsenal has been laid out on the cavernous kitchen island (which is more of a continent than an islands, if the truth be told) for inspection. Eyeing our panoply of recording equipment, Tenney waxes lyrical on the virtues of using both an old-school tape recorder and a digital voice recorder to cast a wider net when trying to capture EVPs.

"Analog reel to reel tape recording works differently," he explains as we gather around the island. Heather nods along as he sketches out the recording mechanisms on a piece of paper. "It's ferro-magnetic. Little iron oxide particles within that little brown strip of tape interact with the magnet in the tape recorder. The wave sound that is imprinted on that tape gets there by a different manner than the ones and zeros used to store it on a digital recorder."

Tenney draws what looks like a staircase on the sheet of paper to illustrate his point. "When a digital recorder records the sound of my voice, it's an ongoing sequence of off/on data points."

Hence the steps on his diagram. Then he draws what appears to be a roller-coaster track, a big, looping sine wave to represent the analog tape, and indicates several points along the track with the tip of his pencil.

"These subtleties, which can turn up on the tape recording, can be lost on the digital version, with its ones and zeroes."

"Digital lacks some of that nuance," I observe, stroking my chin thoughtfully. Tenney nods.

There, in a nutshell, is the most compelling reason for the paranormal investigator to operate magnetic tape recorders and digital voice recorders side by side at the same time.

For decades, John EL Tenney has been making the argument that rather than using the catch-all term "EVP," paranormal investigators should categorize their findings into electronic voice phenomena, direct voice phenomena and analog voice phenomena, to differentiate the means by which they were captured. It's a very salient point, and I encourage any investigator reading or listening to this book to adopt that approach themselves.

"If you get something on a digital voice recorder and I get something on a tape recorder, then we have two different phenomena at work, because the voice isn't being recorded in the same way," Tenney points out. I agree with that, though I would add that it also makes it likely that what's being captured is also more likely to be an actual physical sound taking place in the room at that particular time. It's why running a video camera concurrently with every voice session is a good idea; more than one supposed EVP has been debunked with video footage, when investigators discovered that a rogue yawn or stretch was really the cause.

Heather looks like her head is about to start spinning. To quote my favorite movie, *Star Wars: A New Hope*, she's taking her first steps into a larger world. In her words, when it comes to igniting an interest in the paranormal, we've just created a monster.

"Stop being so *logical*," Jessica snarks, smiling, "and just let it be *weird!*"

Indeed.

Let's go do something weird.

One part of the colossal house we have only investigated once is the gymnasium. It's a large space filled with weight training and cardio equipment. While Jessica is adventuring elsewhere with Toad and Heather, John accompanies us here for an EVP session. Per his standard, we're running both old school cassette recorders loaded with brand new tapes and digital voice recorders.

Rob and John setting up to investigate the gym.

We each take a seat on either the floor or a convenient piece of gym equipment, and John opens the session by greeting anybody who might be in here with us.

"You already know us by now," he begins, "so please understand that nobody here means you any harm. We appreciate how difficult it can be to communicate. If there's anything you want to say, we have devices and machines that will allow us to hear you. We can pass on messages to anyone you may have loved or may need to speak to."

From somewhere up above comes the sound of Heather talking. Tenney tags it for the benefit of the recording and continues on without breaking stride.

"Can you tell us what you see?"

All is silence.

"Can you tell us the name of someone that you cared about?"

Nothing.

"If you don't want to talk, could you move something in this room so that we know you're in here with us?"

A minute passes. Then two. Not a thing moves. The only sound is that of our collective breathing and perhaps a sense of low-grade anticipation.

Tenney decides to switch things up, and coaches us on an EVP gathering technique he refers to as "the Circle." As the name implies, he sets a pair of recorders running, and then ushers all of us into a circle, telling us to take hands with the people on either side of us.

"We're going to all ask the same question," he says, "because in all of my meanderings through this world of weirdness, I sometimes wonder whether they're not hearing our voices at all — rather, they're discerning the *intention* of our question. During most EVP sessions, everybody's thinking up their own question to ask, and focusing on that. It might be a cacophony to them. But, if we all ask the same question and focus on that one thing, we start pushing the question to them, thought-wise."

It's an intriguing idea, one that I've never even considered, and I'm eager to give it a try.

"That is genius," Rob observes. He's right.

Clasping hands loosely with our friends on either side, the group shuffles into more comfortable positions.

"I feel like this is a part of ghost hunting that too often gets lost," Tenney says. "This connection between human beings."

A barking from elsewhere in the building suggests that Toad may finally have met Pork, Beans or Satan.

"Can you tell me the name of someone you love?" Tenney begins.

I leave thirty seconds for a potential reply, and then I repeat the question.

Thirty seconds later, so does Jill...then Stephen...and finally, Rob.

We've come full circle. Tenney begins a new cycle.

"Can you tell me what year it is?"

The rest of us follow suit.

"How many are there?"

It's interesting to note that Tenney doesn't specify how many of *what*.

Another cycle.

"Thank you." Tenney nods respectfully to whomever may have spoken during the session, then leans forward and switches off the recorders. "We used this technique at Ashmore Estates once, in a group of twelve. I asked: *Can you tell me what you see?* There was no response, or so we thought at first...but one girl asked if we could listen to it again. When we did, she turned white. In between her and her mother, who was sitting next to her, asking *Can you tell me what you see?* a male voice could be heard asking the exact same thing..."

Somebody was getting into the spirit of things after all, pun very much intended.

Unfortunately, such doesn't turn out to be the case here at the Blumberg residence. After playing back both the digital voice recording and analog tape, listening to them several times over, no analog or electronic voice phenomena are detected. A shame, but also par for the course, as every member of our group has learned over the years.

The shadows are growing long, and our time is coming to an end. We all head outside, the Blumbergs and my team, to take a group photograph. We cluster in the street outside the funeral home, keeping a watchful eye out for traffic. As soon as the pictures have been taken, I turn around and look up at the third-floor windows and the widow's walk. I'm half expecting to see one of the many spirits staring back at me. Yet this house of secrets seems determined to hang on to a few of them.

I can respect that.

It has been eye opening. It has been at times somewhat chilling. Above all else, it has been tremendous fun. Both the house and the family who occupy it have been absolutely delightful, and as we relive the highlights of our investigation, everybody is in agreement that we need to come back and investigate further. This is a dynamic haunting, something too broad and deep to be neatly summed up in a single investigation, let alone definitively encapsulated between the covers of a single book.

At the end of the evening, hugs are exchanged, and goodbyes are said. We pour ourselves out of the front door, the afterglow of good companionship with new friends is beginning to morph into sadness. None of us wants to leave. We've all grown deeply attached to those who call this place home...both the living and the dead.

From the ground floor windows, three sets of beady eyes watch us go — Pork, Beans and Satan, tails wagging as our car pulls away. The Blumbergs all wave us off, no doubt relieved to get their own space back after the past few days.

Watching the house and family recede in the rear-view mirror, none of us has any idea of the consequences that will result from this investigation. The haunting is about to level up...

Raffterword

O pinion is incidental.

Living in this house of a twisted history I have met a multitude of researchers, both paranormal and not, and faced the term "believer" more times than I can recall. A term sullied by those who disregard skeptics, by those who develop a narrower scope for what is possible than the "non-believers" they try to convince.

Then there is Richard.

Perhaps the only investigator, maybe even the only person I have met who genuinely embodies the title of "believer" because to Richard, the facts overpower preconceived ideas, and every detail opens a door to possibility.

As an amateur skeptic I believe everything is possible, but without a personal experience, it remains a possibility, not an actuality. When Richard Estep first came to our home it was apparent he felt the same. He arrived without expectation or bias, only with a deep passion for learning and deliberation. While his good nature was evident (demonstrated through some of the best/worst dad jokes ever), I was nervous to participate in the carefully curated exercises he had prepared for fear of letting him down through my unfortunate inability to engage with the hidden and strange. But quick was my relief as Richard rejoiced only in the truth and emphasized that all experiences are unique and even silence is a deafening answer.

My experiences with the otherworldly are few and far between, causing my beliefs to be torn. Are the tappings in the hall the settling of a grand old house, or something different entirely? Did I forget to close that door or is something creeping in? Has my delving into the history of this house left me searching for things that aren't really there? It doesn't matter because opinion is incidental.

This house is coated in tragedy and compassion. The facts, terrible and in volumes, are laid out by a man who acknowledges what is assumed, what is felt and what is known. Richard Estep is a man of respect and dignity, holding the truth in the highest regard no matter how mundane or terrible it reveals itself to be.

Rafferty Blumberg
Dresden, Ontario
June 2024

Afterword to the Raffterword

O kay, I confess. I wanted to let Raff have the last word. I really did.

The problem is, his afterword was so complimentary, I didn't want to end the book on that note. As much as I appreciate his very kind words, this story isn't about me. It isn't even entirely about the Blumbergs, as they would be the first to tell you.

It's about the other residents of their home.

The results of our investigation only uncovered the tip of the iceberg. It would be easy to make assumptions about the identity of those who haunt the Blumberg house. Naturally, one tends to assume that because of the location's long association with the funerary profession, many of the spirits stem from that.

This may or may not be the case. Having spoken with several funeral directors over the years (primarily off the record) I learned that strange happenings do occur from time to time, as they perform their essential final service to the departed. However, there is more to the house in Dresden than funerals. It was a family home for many years. Numerous men, women and children called it home — and still do, to this day. They, too, leave their mark. Sometimes that mark is positive...and sometimes, not so much.

A lot can happen in eighteen months.

Noa has begun to connect with some of the child spirits in the house. She has gotten into the habit of sitting on her bed in the evening and sharing the events of the day with them, talking out loud and filling them in on the latest news and goings-on in her life.

Sometimes, usually long after she has fallen asleep, a female spirit talks back to her. Heather awoke one morning at around 2:30am — during that same time window in which the house seems most paranormally active — and could clearly hear the sound of a girl's voice coming from Noa's room. At first, Heather thought that Noa was awake and chatting to a friend on the phone. That in itself would have been unusual at such an early hour. Climbing the stairs quietly, Heather peeked around the door to Noa's room and saw that her daughter was fast asleep.

This began to happen more and more often. The voice is that of a younger girl, possibly in her early teens, but is clearly distinct from Noa's own. Without giving away any personal details, Noa developed a liking from somebody at her school. After revealing this to her spirit friend, Noa went to sleep one night. Heather clearly heard the girl asking: "Is this the first time you've liked somebody?"

True to their word, Heather and Noa have stayed in contact with Pauly. It became a regular occurrence for them to take a Ouija board down to the Speakeasy and spend some time chatting with the kind elderly lady. Pauly still watches over Noa at night, sometimes sitting on her bed while she's drifting off to sleep.

Rather than delving into Pauly's past, the conversation is basically just casual chit chat. Heather likes to ask Pauly's opinion on the current state of the house, finding out whether she likes the decor of a certain room or design project. Pauly is the paranormal equivalent of that sweet auntie many of us have, the one we only get to see on a periodic basis, such as the holidays.

Also active on the third floor is former resident Edward Huston. He may be responsible for the very unquiet night experienced by one of Noa's friends, a young fellow named George, who came to stay for a few days. George slept on the couch in Noa's living area. Perhaps reflecting those Victorian-era social mores and values, the notion that a young man spending the night within close proximity to a young lady (despite the fact that she was sleeping behind a locked door) George was subjected to a night of constant disturbances.

Heavy footsteps stomped around the couch, back and forth, in a circular pattern. There were invisible impacts on the couch, as though somebody was striking it repeatedly with a closed fist or foot. It was even shaken at one point.

"Poor George was *terrified*," Heather recalls. "He didn't get a wink of sleep. Somebody was apparently *pissed* that he was there..."

Understandably, George hasn't been back since.

One of the biggest changes to have taken place since my departure involved Arryn's attitude. Gone is the skeptical stance he adopted during our investigation. Enough strangeness has taken place since then that he has finally come to accept, beyond a shadow of a doubt, that his house truly is haunted.

They say that imitation is the sincerest form of flattery. If so, quite a bit of flattery seems to be taking place within the walls of the old funeral home. Sitting in the living room one evening, Arryn thought nothing of the fact that Raff walked past in the hallway.

"Would you like a drink?" Arryn called out to his son, who was preparing to make one for himself and Heather. There was no response. He called out loudly: "HEY RAFF, DO YOU WANT A DRINK?"

Again, no response. That was odd. Raff is an unfailingly polite individual. Puzzled, Arryn went to find him. An equally puzzled Raff told his dad that he hadn't left his room, let alone walked past the living room in the past few minutes.

Insomnia kept Heather up one night, so she went to the library to read. After a while, Arryn came in to check on her. One of Heather's pet peeves is that whenever her insomnia is bad, Arryn will say: "You should just sleep." Easier said than done, of course. That is exactly what Arryn said to her that night. Choosing to respond with nothing more than industrial grade stink eye, Heather watched her husband turn around and walk soundlessly out of the room.

At least, she *thought* it was her husband.

It was only afterward that Heather realized: she hadn't heard a single sound. No creaking floorboards. No footsteps on the staircase. Nothing. Apart from the one statement he made, the encounter was completely soundless.

Almost eerily so.

Heather went upstairs to their bedroom, and found her husband fast asleep on the bed, snoring up a storm. Moreover, he was completely naked, as he preferred to sleep that way. The Arryn she had just encountered had been fully dressed, wearing a T-shirt and sweatpants.

Arryn doesn't sleepwalk. He and Heather have no good explanation for what happened.

On two other occasions, Arryn has entered the same room in which Heather was sitting, and simply stood there, silently watching her. When she asked what he was doing, there was no response. Heather would turn to look at him, only to find that he had disappeared. On checking with him later, Arryn denied ever having been there.

Audible mimicry has also taken place. On multiple occasions, Noa and her friends have heard what they thought was Heather's voice calling out to them. In reality, Heather did nothing of the sort.

During Christmas of 2023, Arryn's cousin Nick, his partner and their two young children came to stay at the house. Much as Arryn had been, Nick was rather skeptical when it came to the paranormal.

That wouldn't last.

It took one week in the Blumberg household to change his mind. At first, things were quiet. On the second night, the sound of children's footsteps running around the empty hallways. Arryn noted that this was the first time the house had been host to such young children — *living* children, that is — for years.

On the third night, the sound of disembodied laughter — the laughter of children — echoed through the house. A little girl could be heard crying in an empty room.

On the fourth night, at 02:30 in the morning (there's that same time frame again) the home entertainment system switched itself on and began blasting music through the halls and rooms.

"Switching the system on is a whole process," Arryn explains. "You can't do it accidentally. It has to be intentional. It has to be loaded, configured, and the music selected."

Two weeks after Nick and his family left, Heather was away on a business trip. The music began playing again, this time at 02:35, blaring from directly outside the master bedroom door.

Nick had a brief encounter with the male apparition that Heather has seen regularly, this time in the main hallway. The apparition only registered for a brief second before vanishing, one of those "blink and you'll miss it" situations.

Other houseguests have run into the same man during their stay.

"His approach to this at the beginning was kind of where I was when you first met me," adds Arryn. "It was kind of: *I don't NOT believe, but I've also never experienced anything make me believe.* By the end of the week, he had begun to believe."

The main point he wants to emphasize is that the haunting is no longer a Blumberg-only phenomenon. Friends, family, and houseguests have all reported a brush with something otherworldly when visiting the old funeral home. The list of eyewitnesses grows with every passing month.

One night, Heather and Arryn were fast asleep in bed. To that point, the ghosts seemed to have respected their boundaries, leaving the couple alone in their bedroom after nightfall.

Heather awoke in the darkness to find Arryn all but slapping her, trying to get her attention.

"What?" she mumbled groggily, blinking bleary eyes. White-faced, Arryn's eyes were wide and horrified. He wordlessly pointed toward the bedroom doors, which were closed but had a small gap between them. Visible within that gap was a man's face, pressed up against the gap and staring at them...

Their very own paranormal Peeping Tom.

"I don't remember any of this," Arryn recalls sheepishly.

"My hero husband." Heather rolls her eyes. "He rolled over and went back to sleep."

Yet the fact that two of them saw the face strongly implies that this was no dream, trick of the light, or the product of overly active imaginations.

Clearly, in paranormal terms, the house continues to awaken.

Despite its great popularity, at the time of writing (the summer of 2024) *We Bought a Funeral Home* has not been renewed for a second season. Hopefully this will be rectified in the future, as so much of the story remains to be told.

Heather and Noa have continued to connect with the spirits of the house, making time to regularly go down to the Speakeasy and talk to Pauly via the Ouija board. Noa feels comforted to have her own guardian angel — two, if you count her grandfather — watching over her while she sleeps.

In a plot twist that nobody saw coming, the Blumbergs have moved out of the funeral home — temporarily, they hope — due to the necessities of their career. They still retain ownership, and the paranormal activity has never been stronger.

Rather than let the house sit empty and unappreciated (its fate for far too long prior to the Blumbergs moving in) they have made the house available for rent on AirBnB. How much longer this will continue is unknown, but at the time of writing, you, Dear Reader, can spend a night or two experiencing the house for yourself. I strongly encourage you to do so —

— and if the spectral residents of the home should make their presence known to you, please do let us know.

This book may be at its end, but the next chapter of the story is only just beginning, as Heather found out in July 2024 when she was prepping the home for its next AirBnB guest. She has gotten into the habit of leaving a voice recorder running whenever she's alone in the house.

"I really love this house," she remarked, not really speaking to anyone in particular. "In fact, when I die, I'm just gonna come and live here."

On playing back the recording, Heather's comment was greeted with the sound of loud disembodied laughter.

I, for one, agree with the ghosts. It's funny, and I think she's absolutely right.

Gratitude

As with every book I've ever written, many people contributed to this one. First and foremost, I'd like to thank the coolest family in Dresden: the Blumbergs (and Doc) for accepting me and my motley crew into their world and letting me try to tell their story in my own imperfect way. You can learn more about them here:

Heather's Design Services, Appearances and all other Blumberg inquiries: heather@620xst.com

For house rentals on Airbnb: airbnb.com/h/wbafh

Follow The Blumbergs on Instagram: @the_blumbergs

Follow The Blumbergs on TikTok: @the_blumbergs

Raff and Doc's 3D rendering and animation company: Design & Render Projects - Animation, Models (designandrenderpro.com)

Thanks are due to my wife, Laura, who really wanted to accompany me, but stayed home instead to hold down the fort. I know that had to have sucked.

Stephen, Jill, Rob, Brad, Tim, and Jim, you guys were awesome. Thank you for traveling with me to Dresden and helping me delve into the mysteries of this crazy-ass house.

Thanks to the weirdest trio in Michigan, Toad, John and Jessica, for making the trip out to Dresden, and for bringing coffee. Follow their adventures on the What's Up, Weirdo podcast. Find them (and support them) on Patreon at www.patreon.com/whatsupweirdo/ I have it on good authority that, if you happen to be the actor Glen Powell, you can get a free lifetime subscription, but you didn't hear that from me.

Vickie Trickett and Becky Adams, thank you for sharing your perspective and your expertise.

Kat Armstrong, I appreciate you taking the time out to set up a scrying mirror link with us (and yelling at your wee husband to turn the television down).

MJ Dickson, for waiving her diplomatic immunity and remoting in to help.

A big thank-you to my Patreon supporters and readers. Without your support, I would be unable to write about these incredible adventures:

Amy Bruni; Amy Osborne; Ashley Wiseman; Beth Wojiski; Bonnie Gurney; Deborah Schaaf; Elaine Eakes; Elizabeth Rodgers; Jade Harmeyer; Jim Sturgill; Jenna McCreary; Jenny Davis; Jess Canfield; John Howe; Judy Regini; Will and Kat Armstrong; Kathy Beaver; Kayte Robbins; Kelly Kosuda; Kelly Haapala; Kendra Lane; Linda Corbet; Linda Dix; Natasha; Nicole DeYoung; Pamela Thurman; Patrizia Charping; Robbin and Norma Terry; Robin Kruger; Ryan Wefelmeyer; Sara Evraets; Sarah Sullada; Shannon Byers; Sue Ellis-Brown; Susan Cummins; Tammy Hartkopf; Theresa Hathaway; Winona Delgadillo; Thomas Falk; Alison Newell; Alysia Leonhardt;

Andrew Arthurton; Andrew Whittle; Elise; Heath Edwards; Johanna Keohane; Lisa Burgess; Lisa Steffes; Mark Johnson; Meghan Keohane; MJ Dickson and Duncan (chavs on holiday!); Paul Noreika; Rachel Vore Engle; Shari Cain; Terri Allmon; Alex Matsuo; Brian Corey; Connie Mianecki; Jeffrey Lomicky; Justin Stallman; Paul Schmidt; Tracy Pineau.

I appreciate you all.

Until next time, friends...

Made in the USA
Middletown, DE
04 September 2024

59723013R00126